Praying for Strangers

"*Praying for Strangers* will bless you and alter the way you see those seemingly random people that God places daily in your path."
—Ron Hall, *New York Times* bestselling coauthor of
Same Kind of Different as Me

"Extraordinary. *Praying for Strangers* reminds us (through the power of this tiny, seemingly insignificant act) that we can never assume we know the vast universe that exists inside the person next to us—or the one we are yet to discover inside ourselves. I have my next year's resolution."
—Neil White, author of *In the Sanctuary of Outcasts*

"By means of story, anecdote, and calm persuasion, River Jordan suggests an unexpected remedy for both our cultural malaise and our sense of spiritual powerlessness: that we make a habit of praying, not for people we know, but for strangers, in an unheralded, untrumpeted gift of grace. The very act is compelling and quietly subversive in a culture where strangers equal threat and gifts demand notice. And in the end, the gift you might be giving is one to yourself."
—Janis Owens, author of *The Schooling of Claybird Catts*

"I read this book cover to cover and think it will top my gift list for friends and family members. It's a book that, above all else, reminds us of the need for universal kindness."
—*Southern Literary Review*

"Extraordinary . . . Jordan writes eloquently about her experiences and the lessons she learned . . . The idea of praying for strangers is admirable, and a reader looking for inspiration may find hope and grace in this account of the blessings of a prayerful life."
—*Publishers Weekly*

continued . . .

"Will inevitably affect the world of every reader who loses themselves in this memoir's masterfully written pages . . . Spiritual, full of hope, and laugh-out-loud funny, *Praying for Strangers* will have readers cackling through the tears, cheering Jordan's courage, and opening their eyes to the strangers that they rarely pause to meet. Honest, genuine . . . *Praying for Strangers* is an authentic must-read for people in all walks of life." —Examiner.com

"Gently beguiling . . . [a] very personal journey in self-discovery."
—*Booklist*

"Offers readers a wonderfully written, shimmering, accessible, and wholly honest account of a journey into intercessory prayer. It is a journey that more of us might be encouraged to take because River Jordan has been willing to show us how." —*Englewood Review of Books*

"Every once in a while I find a read that is so compelling, I wish that I owned stock in the author. River Jordan made me feel this way as I followed her very personal journey in *Praying for Strangers*. The stories are winsome, the lessons are timeless, and the power of generosity and grace shines ever so brightly each time the page turns." —Pastor Randy Phillips, Seattle, WA

"In a word, River Jordan's book is transformative. *Praying for Strangers* provides us with a wonderful template for a spiritual practice that is accessible to all!"
—Pastor Bob Bauman, Wrightsville United Methodist Church, Wrightsville Beach, NC

PRAYING
for
STRANGERS

An Adventure of the
Human Spirit

River Jordan

BERKLEY BOOKS, NEW YORK

THE BERKLEY PUBLISHING GROUP
Published by the Penguin Group
Penguin Group (USA) Inc.
375 Hudson Street, New York, New York 10014, USA

Penguin Group (Canada), 90 Eglinton Avenue East, Suite 700, Toronto, Ontario M4P 2Y3, Canada
(a division of Pearson Penguin Canada Inc.) • Penguin Books Ltd., 80 Strand, London WC2R 0RL,
England • Penguin Group Ireland, 25 St. Stephen's Green, Dublin 2, Ireland (a division of Penguin
Books Ltd.) • Penguin Group (Australia), 250 Camberwell Road, Camberwell, Victoria 3124, Australia
(a division of Pearson Australia Group Pty. Ltd.) • Penguin Books India Pvt. Ltd., 11 Community
Centre, Panchsheel Park, New Delhi—110 017, India • Penguin Group (NZ), 67 Apollo Drive,
Rosedale, Auckland 0632, New Zealand (a division of Pearson New Zealand Ltd.) • Penguin Books
(South Africa) (Pty.) Ltd., 24 Sturdee Avenue, Rosebank, Johannesburg 2196, South Africa

Penguin Books Ltd., Registered Offices: 80 Strand, London WC2R 0RL, England

While the author has made every effort to provide accurate telephone numbers and Internet addresses at
the time of publication, neither the publisher nor the author assumes any responsibility for errors, or for
changes that occur after publication. Further, the publisher does not have any control over and does not
assume any responsibility for author or third-party websites or their content.

PUBLISHING HISTORY
Berkley hardcover edition / April 2011
Berkley trade paperback edition / April 2012

Berkley trade paperback ISBN: 978-0-425-24560-6

The Library of Congress has cataloged the Berkley hardcover edition as follows:

Jordan, River.
Praying for strangers : an adventure of the human spirit / River Jordan. — 1st ed.
p.   cm.
ISBN 978-0-425-23964-3
1. Prayer. 2. Jordan, River. I. Title
BL560.J67   2011
204'.3—dc22   2010048306

PRINTED IN THE UNITED STATES OF AMERICA

10 9 8 7 6 5 4 3 2 1

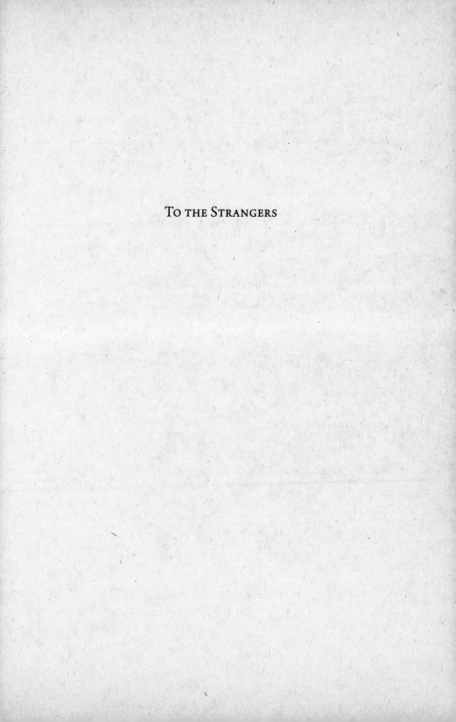

To the Strangers

ACKNOWLEDGMENTS

These people are so pertinent to the full realization of this book. A few from personal history, and some seemingly invisible. Please allow me a moment to shine a light on just a few people to whom I am deeply grateful for their influence on this particular project.

A special thank-you to the memory of my grandmother Estelle, who allowed me to rest my sleepy head when the "preaching" ran long at that little Primitive Baptist Church on a country hill. A special note of gratitude to my mother for introducing our family to the Episcopal Church when I was eleven. It was the perfect place for this young writer to soak up the rhythm of the words spoken each Sunday, to understand a passion of prayer for all people, and to develop a quiet faith. My first official "reading" took place in that little church, although as the introverted child I was, I preferred to remain anonymous and let someone else do the reading for me. Amazingly, it was a prayer I had written at twelve for the soldiers on the Vietnam War front where my father was serving at the time.

My respect and appreciation for my agent, Greg Daniel, who did such an outstanding job capturing the essence of this book at its earliest stage and guiding the manuscript to the perfect home. Denise Silvestro, thank you for your outstanding editing that has somehow tamed my wild words into order with eloquence. My great admiration goes out to the marketing and publicity team at Berkley, including Craig Burke, Rick Pascocello, Melissa Broder, and Erica Martirano—your enthusiasm for these words and their possibilities inspire me. For the Berkley art department, especially Judith Lagerman and Sarah Oberrender.

An ever-grateful heart for my husband, Owen Hicks, who championed this resolution from first whisper, continuously encouraged me to write the words, and championed the book at every turn. And for the generations of my people who have taught me by example that a stranger's story is worth more than my weight in gold.

Dear Reader,

I have written many versions of this letter to you. Picture an old typewriter, a wastebasket overflowing with crumpled drafts, and me huddled yet again, trying to type the words I hold in my heart. What I have to say seems so monumental it leaves me klutzy with the rhythm of my words—feeling hopelessly confused and convoluted in trying to express a simple truth to you. Yet, once again, here I sit, trying to say something vitally important. Please listen closely and forgive me my inability to forge perfectly these thoughts so dear.

By the time you open these pages, I will have been praying for strangers since this resolution began more than three years ago. What started as a spark of an idea became a yearlong commitment; then, instead of ending as neatly as I had planned, it continued. Or rather, I continued. Praying for the lost, lonely, beautiful, aged, famous, and forgotten. As I did so, something happened along the way: I began to change. Slowly. In ways imperceptible. Day by day, stranger by stranger. Somewhere along the way, I woke up. And now everywhere—coast to coast, in cities and small towns, on back roads and sidewalks—readers like you are doing the same thing. They are opening their eyes and hearts to the human condition, caring in a new way, sometimes sharing and sometimes choosing not to, but always remembering one special soul.

Since the publication of *Praying for Strangers*, a multitude of letters and e-mails have found their way to me. The depth of their words, the raw truth, and the heart's cry of how this book you hold has changed them took me by surprise. Now, however, with a year's worth of these stories under my belt, it's no longer such a shock to me. It's much more of an understanding. The experience has affected me the same way. We are indeed in this together.

Three years ago I began this adventure with a resolution in my pocket, a well-meaning but shaky heart, and trepidation in my feet. Presently, my resolution has become a lifestyle. On my best days, my heart overflows with compassion, and my feet . . . Well, they're a little worn but ready. I never imagined that this simple act could touch so many lives, but now *I know it can*. I invite you to join the adventure. I promise you this: Both you and the world will be the better for it.

Yours on the journey,
River Jordan

If you would like additional ways to incorporate the gift of praying for strangers into your life, please consider Praying for Strangers: Twelve Keys in Twelve Weeks at www.prayingforstrangers.com.

Resolution Day

*The great tragedy of life is not unanswered
prayer, but unoffered prayer.*

—F. B. MEYER

M Y SONS ARE MARCHING OFF TO WAR. THAT'S THE ONLY
thing on my mind as we approach the holiday season of 2008. Both of my boys are being deployed at the same
time. One to Iraq and one to Afghanistan. Suddenly the
holidays become critically important. We *have* to be together.
Everything has to be perfect. Because—what if? That's what
I think and don't venture saying. What if it's our last Christmas together? What if it's the last time I see my sons alive?
What if it's the last time I see them together?

Normally I approach the end of the year with a new one
on my mind. By Thanksgiving I am often already considering my New Year's resolutions. Every year I see them as a way
to complete myself, to make up for all those things I haven't
accomplished in a lifetime but can now master in a year.

To better myself by learning three new languages, playing chess, or working out every single day of my life. Each year I fail, if it can be called that. I simply don't carry on because life gets in the way of my enthusiasm to learn Italian "like a spy" or to comprehend quantum physics. I think the reason that these resolutions drop away regardless of my great intentions is because, ultimately, these things don't really have much to do with my real world, my day-to-day living. I'm not lunching with Italian spies followed by an invigorating game of chess as we discuss the possibilities of the reality of this thing called string theory. I need life to meet me at the crossroads of my daily existence, something that shouts back at me from the mirror in the morning. So resolutions, all these beautiful life-growing challenges, turn to dust.

This year it's different. I don't care about resolutions at all. The only things on my mind are the faces of those two young men and them coming home again. I'm not sleeping well at night. I think I've started grinding my teeth. Resolutions are out the window. It's just not the year for them.

Then, out of the blue, a resolution drops down into my spirit. I was standing in my kitchen when it happened. I froze for a moment, the way that old RCA dog looked with his head turned sideways, and thought, *Hmmm.* The idea just dropped right down in my soul the way that maybe a title for a new novel would, or a plot for a story.

New Year's resolution—pray for a stranger every day.

I received that little burst of inspiration the way I do

when a new character shows up in my mind. I might just get a glimpse of a character's face, or hear one line of dialogue and then put that idea up on my writer shelf until I can get around to it. I file this praying for strangers resolution idea right next to that barefoot character that has been sitting on her porch for seven years waiting for me to tell her story. I don't discount it, because the minute that resolution idea crosses my mind, I think of another day when a stranger crossed my path about four years earlier. Her name was Esther.

I was lying on a blanket in Bicentennial Park. A woman approached me carrying a multitude of bags. She talked first to herself, then to me. She approached me and asked if I had a dollar to spare.

"No," I told her, which was true. I'm usually good for a dollar and don't care where it goes. It's not my concern whether the dollar goes to drink or the lottery or warm soup. It's the giving of it that interests me. But on this day I had no dollars to give.

"Not a dollar," I said. "Not a dime."

The woman paused. She looked down at me. I cupped my hands over my eyes to shield them from the sun, and I focused on the shadow of her. She put down her bags and shuffled through her jeans. "Look here," she said. "God have mercy on me when I don't have something to give. Let me help you out." So she pulled out a worn dollar from her jeans, a dollar that had seen some things, and rattled out coins from half a dozen pockets. "For you," she said. I started to protest but she pulled up her pant leg, showed me her metal leg trailed by her metal foot. "Lost it in a wreck," she said. "All I have to do is show people my leg and tell them my story. I'll get a dollar."

No doubt, I thought. And why not? If a metal leg wasn't worth a dollar, then the story of it surely was.

Then she asked me my name—which she liked a lot and told me hers: Esther. I told her I liked her name, too. Then Esther told me to keep the amber in my hair and that I should always wear earth tones. "Listen to what I'm saying now." She searched for a match. "And don't forget, earth tones look best on your skin. You don't smoke, do you?"

"Not anymore."

"Well, you might not believe me, but I know what I'm saying. I know about colors." She gave up on the light and returned the cigarette to her pack, then said, "Reckon God's telling me I didn't need that smoke no way."

As a writer, my life is threaded with story. Those I write, those I've heard as a child, and those I've read. Looking at Esther with her hand out, I immediately thought of the story of a man who once passed a beggar on the street who kept asking for coins. The man finally told him, "I have no coins to offer you. All I have are my prayers, but those I will gladly share." So, I offered to pray for her. It was the least I could do, yes? After all, I was and am a believer. What else could I do for a homeless person with one leg when I had no food or money on me?

To be honest, I don't remember if at that moment I prayed for Esther, for her metal leg, for her riches, or the lack of them. But I remember Esther praying for me. Because she did. A high-and-mighty, somebody-sure-is-listening prayer. A somebody-who-had-read-the-Bible prayer. An open-handed prayer. Esther prayed for this pilgrim with all her homeless heart.

As she walked off, she said, "Remember me in your prayers, River Jordan." Then she praised God for something I couldn't hear and lifted her hands to the sky. For just a moment I watched her go and thought about the stories I'd heard from my grandmother about entertaining heavenly angels unaware. To her, any stranger met along a road could be an angelic being disguised as a human. Someone sent like the gods of Greek mythology to test the human spirit. But Esther looked very real. All real woman, less one leg.

Later, my husband said incredulously, "You took money from a homeless woman?"

"Yes," I said, "and candy, too. Look, she gave me pieces of things." And so she had. Bits of mints and old pieces of gum. I saved them for a long, long time before I finally threw them away. I couldn't explain the logic of that act: me taking money, taking candy, from someone living on the streets and in between them. But logic had nothing to do with it. There was just me and Esther caught in a moment in the park. A simple slice of time where one human being met another and there was that momentary bubble—that moment of stranger-to-stranger acknowledging that we were alive and the same in spite of everything. That we were sisters with stories to tell. That we could pass a few minutes, or even hours, in one another's company and both be the better for it.

Later that night I stepped inside a church and I placed Esther's money in the offering. I wrote her story and her name on the back of the envelope, then paused a moment before turning to leave. I was thinking of how the smallest gift could be counted as the greatest. About how someone offering everything they had, even when it added up to so little, could be the greatest gift of all. Of how Esther's dollar reeked of selflessness. Of an open palm and unclenched hand. And then I prayed miracles for Esther. As I dropped that wrinkled dollar in the offering plate, I prayed the strongest words and images that came to mind.

Some nights Esther's parting words, "Pray for me, River Jordan," echo in my soul. Not every night, but some nights. Particularly on cold nights when I lie in my warm bed before I fall asleep, I remember and I pray, "Lord, keep Esther warm tonight. And give her food, and keep her safe," not always knowing that I have made a difference, but at least hoping that I have.

And all of this comes to my mind in a split second when I hear that phrase—*pray for a stranger every day*. This is what it looks like so I get it. I know what praying for a perfect stranger who crosses your path looks like.

But I'm not real concerned with the Esthers of the world right now. I'm far more concerned about Thanksgiving dinner and Christmas travels, ensuring that we'll all be together in this big cabin in the mountains and that everyone shows up.

Actually, I may be closer to the verge of hysteria than I realize, as I keep saying, "Cost means nothing! Money means nothing! Distance means nothing! We all have to be together!" Well, ask the family; I imagine they would back me up on the hysteria part.

Praying for strangers is not, I repeat *not*, on the top of my list. The only thing on the top of my list is my boys surviving the year and coming home safe. Nothing glorious or saintly about it. Right now, I don't care about anybody else. I'm a little mad about the whole thing. Okay—*a little* is an understatement. I'm mad about all war. I'm mad because I'm not certain about the thinking that got us into these places in the first place. I'm mad that our volunteer army seems stretched to the limits and that the majority of Americans are not emotionally involved in the situation. I'm not a pacifist, and you can't tag me for any political party, so it's not that. I'm just mad. I don't want my sons in a war zone. That's the bottom line, and yes, like my daddy, their great Pawpaw before them who served in Korea and in Vietnam, they are military men. Or at least that's what they are right now and it's what they see when they look in the mirror. But it's not what I see.

I see the first day they rode the school bus alone, I see the first day they learned to ride a bike, when they first learned to whistle, swim, and catch a fish. I'm holding their entire histories in my heart. That's what I see, their entire lives laid out before me. And to think they are being sent to a place that is foreign and hostile, at war with us and with itself, oh brother! And here I am with this foggy notion of a resolution in the back of my mind, one where I'm going to pray for people I don't know and don't care about.

My plate is already full in 2009 with two sons on active duty and deployed, with a family that has their own special needs and prayer requests, with a new novel debuting, travels scheduled, and new deadlines to meet. Oh, and did I mention two sons being deployed? Sure I did. But to be honest, that's how often it circles around in my brain. Just about every other breath at this point. Pray for a stranger—*indeed*. *I* need prayer and a whole lot of it just to keep breathing and moving, to keep up with my life and take care of my people. I am not feeling like Mother Teresa, not too altruistic, and not too holy at all. I am tired, busy, and carrying a double portion of my own concerns.

I venture toward the New Year with a silent mantra— it's all about the family, the family, the family. Oh yes, and me trying to ensure that picture-perfect holiday. One that will make memories that literally last a lifetime. For the first time in our family life, we are meeting at a ski resort in the Blue Ridge Mountains. My best buddy cousin is driving Mama up from North Florida. My sister has scheduled time off and is packing up the niece and nephew. My oldest is packing the family up and heading to the mountains, too. My youngest, already being processed at Fort Dix, is getting Christmas leave and is flying down to meet us in Nashville so that we can join this strange, scattered convoy and converge on that mountain in a holy moment of togetherness bliss.

When I say I hold my sons' histories in my heart, I mean that the way that all mothers would. It's how we see our children, not only as they are, but all the ways that they used to be. For Christmas, I have painstakingly gone through old photograph albums. The kind that are so old-fashioned they were taken back when cameras had something called film. I choose many, many and take a bag stuffed full of photos to be copied. It's my Christmas present to my sons. Picture books of who they used to be. Pictures of them together and growing up. Now, I know full well they may just roll their eyes at their sentimental mother, but I am determined for them to—what? Remember. Relive if only for a moment. Connect as brothers not the way men do but the way boys do who are building forts, riding bikes, and growing up in one another's shadows. Belonging to me and to each other in a way they no longer do because they are men now.

The trip isn't going exactly as planned. The nephew is

sick, and my sister has to stay behind and keep him well. We try to caravan and become separated and lost. And then a horrible thing happens. Our beloved Aunt Kate, my mother's last living sibling, passes away as we are en route to this gathering. We think about the season that we are in and we all talk about it, about the fact that both "boys," as we refer to them in the family, are being deployed. And then we don't say all the things about that that we are thinking. We never do. My mother bravely musters on, continuing toward the Blue Ridge, knowing that after this reunion she will face the heaviness of her sister's funeral. We all eventually arrive late, tired, heartbroken, and overjoyed to be together.

But strange things are happening even as my mind is heavy with events around me. I began watching people in stores as we stop along the way. I begin toying with this New Year's resolution idea. What I see overwhelms me. That grandmother over there trying to make it on those old, tired feet in the freezing cold. That little kid that looks like he's wearing hand-me-down clothes and destined to live a hand-me-down life. That mother slowly counting out her money in the checkout line, nervous that she has too little. Even that man that looks like he has everything money can buy yet his face is pinched with worry. In thinking about this strange resolution thing, I'm wondering—if I even decide to do it—how can I possibly choose just one person? From the looks of things, *everyone* needs prayer. Not just me and my sick nephew, my grieving mother, and the sons heading for two different war zones. Everyone.

I simply tuck this idea away and watch people—and then get back to what is consuming me. I'm calling my cousin in Georgia (thank God for cell phones) and crying with her as I put on lipstick and a brave face for my mom. I'm relishing a fireplace in the woods and being surrounded by these sons of mine. The sounds of my tiny granddaughters playing with my niece. And yes, if it's not a bittersweet Christmas, I don't know what is.

So it hasn't been a picture-perfect trip thus far, but I get my moment. The boys open their little presents jokingly saying, "What, Mom? You gave us another one of your books?" Then they discover these little photo albums filled with images of them. Babies they once were, these men. Baby brothers. My babies. And now they are standing next to one another, turning pages and looking over one another's shoulders and laughing and telling stories. "Remember the time . . ." one says, and the other one answers, "Oh, that was *my* Ninja Turtle, you hear me, not yours and . . ." I look up to see my husband watching me as I'm watching them and he's smiling. He knows this precise moment is my greatest Christmas present. He knows right now it's my forever and it's fighting off any images of a future without them. Resolutions are a thousand miles away.

Life can be funny sometimes. The kind of funny that is strange. Sometimes circumstances force you to face the very thing you are determined to ignore. Something that basically says, *Oh, no you don't. You're not backing out or forgetting about what you are supposed to do. So right in the middle of your self-centered, very busy, and, understandably, highly emotional life, you are still going to focus on something, someone, beyond you.* That's what life says to me with just one chance encounter the next day at a ski resort. It leaves me no options, no second guesses, and no escaping it. I will embrace this praying for strangers resolution with all my might. It will be the first resolution I've ever kept.

BLUE SHOES

Prayer moves the hand that moves the world.

—JOHN AIKMAN WALLACE

W E'VE SPENT THE NIGHT AT THE SKI RESORT CATCHING up and sharing belated Christmas presents. We opened the gifts, had a meal, and everyone was finally nestled in their respective beds. But now it's the official ski day where people are actually supposed to leave the cozy, fireplace-heated cabin and venture forth to strap on skis and sail down the mountain. An unlikely occurrence for me. I look like Lucy Ricardo on skis. So my family, realizing my physical aptitude and athleticism, have asked me to take on the all-important job of holding down the designated spot for people to meet up with one another. A table in the cold. So I sit in the sun, bundle up, and read my book. Occasionally I glance up to look around at the people just for a dose of distraction, and then I'm back to the words. I have a serious job, repeating all day, "This table is taken." I don't mind because we are all together. And that's the important thing. I'll stake out our table in the freezing cold till the cows come home.

As I sit and read, I occasionally consider the fact that it is December thirty-first. I realize that tomorrow is supposed to be my big resolution day. This . . . *whatever it is* . . . this experiment in human kindness and spiritual enlightenment. I have no idea how it's going to work. I still don't feel very kind, spiritual, or enlightened. But dang, it won't go away. Like a determined mosquito, it keeps buzzing in my brain.

After holding our table down for hours, I am finally relieved for a bathroom break by someone covered in snow and holding a snowboard. I stop reading and move through the resort. I don't like this place because it is very crowded. I don't like crowds. The restaurants are packed and overflowing. Everyone talks too loud, and that bothers me, too. I wait my turn *forever* for the restroom, and even then, as I'm in line, I'm mulling over this New Year's resolution.

I'm finally in the restroom, but soon enough I hear a strange noise in the stall next to me. It's a thud of some kind—a banging—followed by a child's cry. I'm expecting the sound of a mother's calm and caring voice saying, "Oh, so sorry, sweetie," or, "Are you okay?" Instead I hear, "Oh, shut up." Then the woman proceeds to yell in a loud voice, "It's always something with you, just go!" And this little voice says, "But I don't need to." There's another sound of something, my guess is something painful, and the child cries out. Someone from outside asks a question I can't quite make out and the woman says, "Everything's fine. He's just the problem. He's always a problem." And there is a tussle and more words next to me and I look down to see two very small feet in blue shoes. The child cries out again and says, "This is why I don't like you."

Let me tell you something true: As a storyteller, I'm a master of dialogue. Of listening to it and capturing it. Finding the truth in it. This statement by the child is not angry or petulant. It is a confession, an attempt to bridge a communication problem that has gone terribly wrong. The woman says, "Yeah, well, I don't like you either, and I'm not ashamed to say so, or for anyone to hear me."

There are a few things I can recognize beyond dialoguing. Child abuse is one of them. Kids get in trouble, they get tired, they get spanked. I'm not on the no-spank team. I was raised in the South, where spankings were a part of growing up. Not beatings, not abuse, just spankings. Of which I think I received two in my whole life. But this child is being abused. And I know it.

All of this happens in the shortest of time spans. I'm thinking I'll walk out the door and the woman will be forcing the child's hands under hot water, briskly washing and shoving. I'm going through the possible scenarios. How to summon the authorities in a crowded ski resort, how to detain the woman, how to just make conversation with her. How to snatch that child out of her arms and run.

I exit the stall. There is no small child in blue shoes at the sink or anywhere else. I run out of the bathroom, search the crowds, the smiling faces in the restaurant, the large gatherings of families filled with children, but those tiny feet are nowhere to be found. I feel responsible. Like I have failed that child, that little stranger that crossed my path, in a thousand ways. I go back to my waiting area to meet up with family and I think of the date. Of how my resolution doesn't officially start until tomorrow. And I carry that little boy in blue shoes with me throughout the day like a box in my heart. I keep my eyes open and searching. Even later, when we leave the ski slope and venture down the mountain for lunch, I search for blue shoes.

Later that night I tearfully tell my husband the story. How I should have done something, anything, to save him.

He says, "Looks like you found your stranger for today."

"It's not the first of the year yet. Not resolution day," I tell him. But of course I've already been praying for the child.

"Don't worry," he adds, "that woman is too loud and too volatile. She's going to get noticed where she can't disappear in a crowd. She's going to get reported."

He's right about that, but I think of that tiny, shaking voice and I wonder what that child is going through at that very moment. And I pray fervently.

Then I think about the power of prayer—of what we do or don't believe about it. If we truly believe that prayers can influence the outcome of lives, then where is our faith, in season and out of season? Where is mine? I'm the kind of woman that really would snatch a child from abusive arms and worry about the consequences later. But am I the kind of woman that can offer up a heartfelt prayer and believe that help is on the way? That it will be speedy and mighty in its deliverance? Believing this way seems so much more challenging to me than taking immediate and physical action.

I wasn't looking for any type of confirmation that my resolution was right and true but I received it. The clock turns over into the New Year. I wait up and watch the ball fall on Times Square with a new awareness. Here are my sons entering into one of the most dangerous years of their lives, one that will consume my life with thoughts of them, and yet, at the same time, there are strangers in my path who need the simplest thing I have to offer, almost as if their lives depend on it. And maybe for some of them they do. And for a few hours, as the year turns over, the most important thing in my life or on my mind isn't myself or my own. It is the earnest prayer for the life of a little stranger.

THE BUS STOP

He will regard the prayer of the destitute.

—PSALM 102:17

THE HOLIDAYS HAVE BEEN LONG. IT SEEMS WE'VE BEEN ON the road forever. First for our big holiday family get-together and then followed closely by Aunt Kate's funeral. In the middle of all of it, I've kept praying. Somehow I've managed to cross paths with a person in a gas station, a motel, a restaurant, who stood out to me in such a way that I knew a silent prayer might help the situation they were facing.

One of the best parts of our holiday has been having my mother-in-law visit. She's more than my husband's mother; she is also my friend, and having her with us is truly a joy. But now she has made up her mind to go home and is determined in her most stubborn way to ride the bus. "I can read," she tells me, "and knit. And there's always the most interesting people to watch." Uh, yeah, I bet. I'm more than a little worried about her and thinking this is the last time we'll give in and relent to her wishes.

We arrive at the bus station and it's crowded. People seem to be tired before their journeys have even begun. I'm watching the crowd as we stand in line to pick up the ticket and shepherd Mother Nancy onto her correct bus.

I need a stranger, I'm thinking like some stalker moving through a sea of bodies, bags, and worn-down suitcases. I guess I *am* stalking, searching in my spirit, thinking, *surely here—somebody.* An older woman with dark hair comes up and speaks to us a few times, and to the lady in front of us. It's gotta be her because if you could see her, you would understand why. Hands down, put my money on it, it's her; she looks like she really, really needs prayer. But is that what I'm really doing here? Am I just supposed to pray for everyone that crosses my path who looks like they could use it? Well, maybe so in the big scheme of things, but this is all about that resolution and I'm still trying to figure it out. I could pray for practically every stranger who crosses my path who looks like he or she needs prayer and I'd have a very busy prayer life. This is different. I feel like I'm supposed to be sensitive to *one significant, special person* every day. Finding that one person is like searching for a needle in a haystack. Particularly at this moment in the Nashville bus station. But then two things happen at the same time.

A woman waiting at the other counter for her ticket pricks my heart. She doesn't look particularly needy, but

I just know she's my stranger. So far, I have accepted this resolution thing, and I've been carrying it out. Silently and to myself. But right now I feel I am not only supposed to pray for her but to *tell her* that I am praying for her.

Great. Just great. Let me give you just a little background on how this new urging affects me.

I am very much *not* an evangelist. Not when it comes to my faith. I'll stand on corners and preach about reading or having a library card, but when things turn to God, I pretty much turn silent for the most part. Let me put it to you this way, if you getting into heaven depended on me being a witness to you on the street, your chances wouldn't be too good. Some people have this gift, but not me. I'll talk to you about the weather, what's on your iPod, the latest TV show, or today's news, but I won't talk about Jesus. And that's not because I don't believe in Jesus, because, just for the record and while we're on the subject—I do. But then I also think that's my business and you'll find your way to God in your way in due time. I sure don't want any part in that or the responsibility for you. So let's be perfectly clear, talking to people about the fact that I am praying for them pretty much turns my stomach and scares me silly. In spite of this, I take a deep breath and tell my husband to wait just a minute because I have something I have to do. I return to the counter where the woman is still waiting on her ticket.

I approach her slowly, not wanting to frighten her. I am well aware that just walking up to people in public and saying, "Excuse me—today you're my stranger," could seem a little peculiar. The fact that I could be pegged as crazy isn't lost on me. I clear my throat and speak to the woman in a low voice so the girl at the counter can't hear us. I tell her about my resolution, explaining that today she is my stranger, that I'll be thinking about her and saying special prayers for her all day. Then the oddest thing happens. She looks at me with what I must call wonder. She grabs me and hugs my neck. "Do you know what I was just saying to God this morning? Do you? I was just praying this morning and praying for other people, but I stopped and asked the Lord, *"God, is there anybody in this whole wide world who is praying for me?"*

Well, what do you know? "Looks like I am," I say and return her hug. "You have a good journey home," I tell her.

"Oh, now I will!" She's wearing a big smile and I can understand why. God answered her question. Looks like he used me in the process.

I return to my mother-in-law, see her safely sitting right behind the driver, and watch the bus pull off with tears in my eyes. I'm feeling a little emotional, about her leaving and about that woman heading in the opposite direction to Kentucky. My husband asks me, "Where'd you go?" I tell him the whole story. He's as amazed as I am and says, "You better write that down."

This incident at the bus station is the true measure that lets me know I'm not just forging some social experiment. Not just trying to break out of my mold of wasted resolutions that never make the grade. I feel I've tapped into something tangible and real, realizing there is a purpose larger than I am. Okay, then purposes are fulfilled. Today has a warm sense of humble satisfaction. My prayers are worth something to a stranger. And now that stranger is worth something to me.

COCKTAIL PARTY PRAYERS

Whoever in prayer can say, "Our Father,"
acknowledges and should feel the brotherhood
of the whole race of mankind.

—TRYON EDWARDS

IT'S BEEN A BUSY DAY IN ATLANTA. BOOK EVENTS AND RADIO program production have kept me occupied throughout the day speaking on panels and interviewing other authors. In the midst of signing books, meeting readers, fielding questions on publishing and the creative muse, I haven't forgotten about praying for someone. I've kept my eyes open, my spirit aware, but even if I had happened to pass someone that I felt I should talk to, carving out a moment to speak to them in private would have been difficult. I don't think I've been alone for five minutes. Now, it's late in the evening and my husband is escorting me to a final cocktail party reception for all the authors at a local art gallery.

After this kind of a long day with a lot of extroverted

conversation and socialization, I've tried to remain sensitive to that special face in the crowd, but now I'm finally relaxing. Still, there are a multitude of author friends to speak to and catch up with. Book festivals are something akin to a high school reunion for writers who have developed friendships, as we only see one another for the most part when we are on the road. Parties such as this one give us an opportunity to share a glass of wine and talk about how the latest writing project is coming along and how the children are doing.

Little by little, I've forgotten that the long day has become late night, and I still haven't prayed for a stranger. But then I pass a woman in the crowd and there she is—just like that. This is a face I recognize to some extent. She knows me as a writer. I know she was in the audience at my panel today, but I don't know her personally. I'm on my way upstairs to view the art exhibit and I think to myself, *I'll talk to her on the way back down.* Then, just that quickly, I forget. By the time I come downstairs again, she isn't there.

My husband and I visit with authors, have dinner, wander through the room making small talk and sharing stories of our recent travels. We finally meander to the wine bar and get in line. The woman in front of me turns around—it's her. That face, that same woman I was meant to pray for. All at once I realize I *have* to talk to her and pull her aside to share that she is my stranger for the day.

"How bizarre," she says, but she is saying this with a light in her eyes. "How really bizarre. Do you know what today is?" She smiles at me, but it's a smile touched by sadness.

Of course I don't know the significance of today other than the big book event. I just shake my head no.

"It's the forty-fourth birthday of my daughter who just passed away. This is the first birthday I've had without her."

How bizarre indeed. We step farther away from the crowded bar and over into a pocket that is a little quieter where we can talk for a while. All the cocktail chatter goes on behind us, all around us. Publishing news, new book titles, announcements of recent events. But right now I'm focused on the woman in front of me, and we talk as one woman, one mother, to another. My husband has drifted away from us. He's become accustomed to this, me stepping to the side, whispering to strangers. The noise of the cocktail party continues to circle us, but we remain in this space as if there is a shield around us. Marsha tells me things about her daughter and about the life she lived. About signs and wonders she has seen since she passed. Little things that have meant so much to her to get her through this.

A parent should never have to bury her child. I want to tell God that should be a rule. But I'm not the rule maker.

"You have a gift," she tells me.

"Oh, I don't know about that. Just following through on this resolution."

"No, it's a gift. And I can't wait to go home and call my other daughters, her baby sisters, to let them know about this. They've been so worried about me that they've been calling all day to see if I'm okay."

She looks at me and smiles in such a way that I know she is going to be okay. That tomorrow will be a little brighter, a little less painful for her. I'm happy she appeared and reappeared. Happy that I let this resolution business take hold of me and that, in spite of all my reservations, I began telling people they had stood out for a reason to me and that I would be praying for them. I'm happy about what this news will mean to those girls. It solidifies my faith in something bigger than me and my daily issues. I don't have a gift any more than the next person. We all have the same gift, the same opportunity. How much does it really take for any of us to slow down to attune ourselves to the human condition, to look for another soul passing through our little universe that might need a word of encouragement?

The birthday of a daughter passed? The safety of a son survived? Our paths cross in this magical, amazing, bittersweet life. If only we knew how important we are to each other. Even as—particularly as—strangers.

A Wellspring of Prayers

We never know the worth of water till the well is dry.

—THOMAS FULLER

H E WAS JUST A GUY IN THE BACK OF A PICKUP TRUCK. BY back, I don't mean the backseat of a crew cab. I mean the back of the truck. I was driving past the truck when our eyes met. I knew. My stranger. One more stranger in what has become a never-ending line. Some days I wonder should I get to heaven, should the gate be tall and wide, should there be any everlasting ground (for the record, I believe these sorts of things), will they be there? Will there be a long line of unknown souls, people I have prayed for in passing? Well, if so, perhaps we'll have a little more time than a brief whispered word.

But for now, what I have is this young man in a truck. I smile and wave to him. Not a glorious wave, mind you. Not a parade wave. Just a raised hand which of its own accord seems to speak *Peace*. He smiles back, raises his hand, and in that moment when our eyes meet, there is a human connection made that escapes any logical bonds or bounds. It triggers a well of compassion, a caring that normally I don't have with every person I pass on a given day. And in that moment I care very much about the young man in the truck. I care that he has a job, and a future, and his destiny is fulfilled. I care about the family that he cares about. For a moment, he is my brother in every sense of the word.

I stop at a red light; the truck stops, too. The young man is to the left of me, just ahead a bit, and he is still looking back at me. I make eye contact again and nod my head and he nods back, then the truck is pulling away and turning left and he raises his hand again to say good-bye. I return the wave and then he's gone. But the gate that has been opened with his appearance doesn't easily close. The wellspring of emotion, that passion of caring, has been released so that I say a blessing for him with tears in my eyes and with all I can muster. And the next thing I know, I am praying for strangers all down the road. That old man standing on the corner, and the woman walking with that burden, and that crumpled-over soul at the bus stop. That could be, I think, me—broken and crumpled and lost instead of living this life of mine. And I pray.

When I grew up in North Florida, my grandparents had what you might call the tiniest mini-farm in the world. Only a few acres but it had pigs, chickens, honeybees, and crops planted. One of the most important things on the farm was the pump that ran the water up, and what we were taught at a very early age was: You must always prime the pump and never let it run dry. Never. So there was always a cup of water left that the former person had pumped out in antici-pation of the next person's visit.

Pumps have been used in stories and allegories for years for good reason. When our pumps run dry as writers, mothers, wives, husbands, fathers—you name it, whether personal or career-wise, it is so difficult to get the flow running smoothly again. The same can be said for prayer, except I would expect that after praying for so many people since this resolution began, my pump was well primed. You would think. But this young man's unexpected appearance, the compassion of my prayer for his life, has opened up a floodgate of prayer. And I wonder what my life would look like if I lived this way, walking and breathing out prayers. Blessings and peace and prayers and wonders and miracles for all that I encounter. I wonder what the city would look like if we all did that, if the world was one big cup of prayer for one day. Only one day. I wonder.

A Broken Man

I KNOW HOW TO PRAY WITHOUT MOVING MY LIPS, MY FACE AS stoic as the rocks of the desert. Unmoving and unmoved. But let my heart sit next to a broken man and brush up against his pain and my face, my prayers, all come unglued. I'll reach out and shake a dirt-caked hand. You should know that about me.

Charles is his name, he tells me with a flat-line face. If there was emotion there once, it's been erased over time and through trial. He's a bulk of unhappy. I try to tell him he is my special person, and I shake his practically lifeless hand. And then I ask him if he has a special prayer request, any prayers held close to the vest he might like to share. He is sitting in a French bakery where I've gone to relish a good hot cappuccino and a little laptop business. It's a perfect writer's world.

But here is this man, not carrying a book bag, not lost in

the latest national paper, not clicking on laptop keys, but just sitting, staring vacantly at the large void of his life before him. I'm still trying to cheer him up. I swear, as lost and dejected as he appears, I think I'd drop into my most horrible version of *Riverdance* if it would get him to smile. "Hopeless," he says, churning up echoes of the Old Testament stories of King Solomon from the book of Ecclesiastes. It's the same book that inspired the Peter, Paul, and Mary song "Turn, Turn, Turn." The ordering of the seasons is a nice poetic piece of King Solomon, but it isn't long before he seems depressed with life and where his decisions have brought him, stating, "All is vanity." I've always thought King Solomon could have used a little of Annie popping up from the Broadway musical at that moment singing the "Tomorrow" song.

"Really, anything special, Charles, you'd like prayer for?"

He shrugs his shoulders. "It won't matter anyway."

Vanity, I hear again, All is vanity and man is but a breath of wasted grace. Okay, my paraphrasing Ecclesiastes lacks a little, but the dark and dreary mood is there.

This man is the most down-and-out case of hopeless I've ever seen and I've known a few. I go to the register to buy him lunch and to just have them send it over anonymously. Maybe a bowl of soup and a sandwich will lure his soul back into the land of the living.

"Oh, for Charles?" they ask and nod toward the sad shape of him. "We've got him covered."

I'm delighted to witness this act of humanity, for a restaurant to care and cater to one so lifeless and forlorn. I guarantee their generosity doesn't provoke him into saying a lot of thanks. He's not wandering the streets spreading cheerful, good words about their establishment. They aren't doing it for the kudos.

"It'll get better, Charles," I tell him from the small adjoining table to his.

He shrugs again. "Probably not."

I sit back and take a sip of my coffee and consider Charles's life. Maybe he is right. Maybe this is the best it's ever going to get for him. Or maybe after a long and unknown story of one pain only leading to another, this is the best it ever has been. The kind of life where a man learns to shut down his expectations and just lives in a state of blank.

Maybe he has prayed before and feels his prayers weren't answered. I know that feeling. I don't know why some prayers are not answered any more than anyone else does. And sometimes I feel like a fool. Maybe we all do when we have prayed with all our might and gumption for a healing, a situation, a marriage—and it didn't stir the waters. We wonder if our prayers are not strong enough or if we aren't good enough—whatever—mothers, daughters, sons, and bosses. Where does the judgment of ourselves begin and our judgment of God end? We want answers. If there were a better formula for prayer, a secret concoction that will render it more effective, what would it be? Fasting, praying on knees, being certain you have a speckless heart with no hidden allergens of hateful residue remaining. I have fasted and have kneeled. I have only managed total forgiveness of all the "someone-did-me-wrong" feelings in my soul for about thirty seconds, fourteen years ago on a Tuesday night. (For me, the art of forgiveness passes like a hot stone. I pick it up again and hold it for as long as possible but it gets away from me some days. Most days.)

There are times I am riddled with shadows of uncertainties. Where are those prayers going anyway? But one thing stands true in my heart—a gift I think from birth. I believe. In the innermost core of my being, I believe there is a great, mighty, and benevolent God who hears my prayer. I don't question how other people get to God, to walk a journey of faith out in their own lives. My faith is personal. I hope theirs is very personal as well. Whatever those beliefs may be on any given day, perhaps they are wondering as I am— *Exactly where are my prayers going anyway?* But my experiences with the divine in the encounters I am making with people of all faiths or no faith at all remain as strong as the things that puzzle me.

But even with my faith, and all the faith of friends who believe differently, taken into account, there remain the eternal questions: Why do some prayers seem to be answered and others not? Why are there tragedies in this world? Sins and crimes rendered against the old, the young, the peaceful, the helpless? I don't know but I tell you what, this old messy life—utopia it ain't.

Still, I believe in God—and I believe in prayer. Color me crazy. I'll just keep praying.

He worried me some, this Charles. I leave with that dark place of him tucked somewhere inside of me. His "pray if you want but none of it matters"—I get that, I get the hopeless end of the rope. I've been there more than once and only by the grace of God found my way out of that dark tunnel, that miry pit. My prayer now is for a miracle of that grace to flood this man. For his latter days not to go this way. And maybe for him to have one good trusted friend. One is all it really takes to help. Someone who can help him chuckle softly at the absurdity of it all.

New Friends in
Kitchens

Rich is the person who has a praying friend.

—JANICE HUGHES

THIS RESOLUTION IS STILL SO NEW I DON'T KNOW HOW TO touch it. I'm never certain what to say to someone or not in any given situation. Even to friends, old and new, the resolution doesn't become public knowledge. It isn't something I discuss. Some of that may be a kind of writer's training where if you talk about a fiction story, you won't write it. You end up telling someone and then someone else and then their friends, followed by all the people you meet at a party, and the next thing you know, there is no story. It's just leftover jokes and anecdotes from the last place you went to visit.

This resolution business is too sacred for that. I don't want friends to say, "What, are you crazy?" I don't want too many questions or even supportive ideas. I just want to keep doing it, to somehow manage to put one spiritual foot in front of the other one day after day. I don't want some strange spiritual hoodooyouvoodoo checklist to pop up and tell me how to do this. I don't even want myself to get into a routine of doing what I do so that it becomes such habit it's more rote than real.

Yesterday, I was in Jefferson, Texas, for a major book event with the notoriously talented Pulpwood Queen founder, Kathy Patrick. I'm having dinner with new author friends in a small café and we are full of conversation about books, publishing, and the importance of book clubs. Our waitress is my new stranger for the day, but it certainly isn't something that I'm going to tell her in front of other people.

It's a casual spot, a place that specializes in great burgers and homemade pies of all varieties. Throughout our dinner I've been watching the waitress, watching her as she refills iced teas and delivers the blue plate special. I finally ask her name.

"Carly," she says.

We finish our meal and I offer to leave the tip.

"Are you sure?" my new friends ask.

"Oh, yeah. I got this one," I tell them, and indeed I do. Sometimes a prayer is just a prayer. Sometimes it's a little something more.

We pay our bills but then I tell my friends I'll meet them

later at our event and leave in search of our waitress, Carly. I find her in the kitchen, where we find a quiet corner for a moment. I give her the tip, which is probably as much as our three bills put together, but it still isn't a lot, I assure you. Burgers and pie don't add up to big bucks, and it's a great deal anyway.

"Oh, are you sure?" she asks me, ready to give the money back.

"Yes, I'm sure. And here's the thing. Every day I pray for a stranger that stands out to me and today you're my person. I'm just going to be thinking about you, I'm going to say an extra prayer for you tonight."

"Oh, you just don't know how much I appreciate that." She gets teary-eyed and I try not to get teary-eyed with her. It's funny how the big tip, although appreciated I could tell, is not the thing that touches her so deeply or moves her to tears. It's the knowledge that somehow she has been singled out, that an extra prayer from an unknown stranger is being said on her behalf. Then she tells me her story. "We've been having a hard time. I live with my grandmother and we try to get by, but it's been tough, you know? Business has been slow." She looks around the restaurant at the empty seats. It's not hard to calculate that empty tables equal empty pockets. I give her a hug, it's an easy thing to do in the Deep South, and tell her I understand.

Then a happiness that I didn't possess walking in prevails as I gather my bag to leave. I won't lie. There's just a touch of satisfaction when someone receives the promise of a prayer. There's a sense that I got something right in the middle of another messy day filled with spilled coffee, lost keys, crumpled pages. It really is a grand thing to pray for people, to give them an extra tip if you're led to, to pass on a good word of encouragement.

I leave Carly with her pocket a little fatter, a special story to share when she gets home to her grandmother, and a smile that's definitely a little brighter. Maybe this resolution thing isn't going to be such a hard thing to do after all.

UNCONDITIONAL LOVE

**Prayer is translation. A man translates himself
into a child asking for all there is in a
language he has barely mastered.**

—LEONARD COHEN

THERE ARE PLACES THAT CAN UNNERVE ME EVEN WHEN I AM
there with the best of intentions. Let's just say one of
those might be a Saturday afternoon birthday spot of thousands of small children. Okay, maybe there weren't thousands but the noise in the place would have one believe it.
Little happy, screaming faces everywhere. Two of those faces
were my niece and nephew, whom I normally refer to as Miss
Fancy and Mr. Smarty because they are just that. It is my love
of these two and my niece's birthday that have driven me
right into the middle of this madness. I am not wearing ear-
plugs or an iPod. Ill prepared, I stare at my sister over a table
full of presents and yell something about, "Why couldn't you
just have a little party?" "You want pepperoni?" she replies.

A really quiet little party would have been fine to me, but this is coming from a strange child who refused to sit with the other kids at her own birthday party when she was five. One who walked out of the room when they started singing "Happy Birthday" to me because I really didn't want all that attention and didn't require the interaction with other children to be happy. True story; ask my mother. She was the one that had to find me and talk me into going back into the room to attend my own party.

But today it's not my party, it's my niece's, and no one asked me how quiet the affair should be. I check my watch and we just arrived. It's going to be a long event. The waitress appears to take the pizza order, and in the middle of all that radical, nerve-jangling noise, I get that slow-motion feeling. No, that doesn't really happen. There are no special effects to accompany my intuition. Just the face of a young girl that I'm now watching make her way through the crowd teeming with children, parents, prizes.

I whisper to my sister and husband, "Back in just a moment," and follow her through the crowd. The niece and nephew are oblivious to my whereabouts.

The girl is maybe sixteen. Who knows or can really tell anymore, but it's a good guess. She's beautiful, no doubt, but right now that beauty is hidden slightly under a polyester uniform, her hair pulled up and back tightly away from her face. She's standing at the drink machine filling up another pitcher full of soda when I approach her. Sometimes my

Southern voice is a good thing. Sometimes the accent can roll up off my tongue heavy enough to soothe somebody's soul the way that I'd want it to soothe mine, calm my nerves.

"Hi, honey," I say and ask her name. I'm always asking names. Maybe it just gives me time, gives them a chance to say something familiar or to think, "Perhaps this person is harmless, thinks that she knows me." Maybe it's the momentary icebreaker that I need. I use it all the time, every day. And then I try to remember the name, to write it in a notebook, to pore back over it and remember the face. It's the faces that surface and remain. Always.

"Shannon," she says.

Then I have to take a deep breath and look around, tell her that I know she's busy but that I do this thing, this resolution, and that every day . . .

She's a serious girl. It's all over her face, her demeanor. She is appreciative and thankful. When I ask her if there is something special she'd like a prayer for, she bows her head a moment, then lifts it and responds with a solid answer.

"My mother. I'd like you to pray for my mother. She's really under a lot of pressure now about everything."

We speak a few more minutes, ever so briefly, but the clock is ticking. She has pizzas in the window and thirsty children at tables.

My husband asks me on the way home, "The waitress, was that your stranger?" He's so used to my disappearances now, to my stories I come carrying home.

"Yeah."

"I thought so because of her bruises."

I look at him. "What bruises?"

"The bruises on her face and arms. Didn't you see them?"

I remember a dark spot, thought it was maybe a birth-mark. Just the colors of her skin. "No, I didn't see them."

"I thought that was why you chose her."

I'm quiet for a little while thinking of Shannon's response, of her request for her mother, for the woman that was under so much pressure that, I now realized, she was probably taking it out on the child that was asking for prayer on her behalf. Not for herself. Not for deliverance or vengeance—but for her mother's stress, her mother's pain, to be lightened.

"I don't think I ever really choose anyone." The choosing remains a mystery to me. People pass in front of me, and like reflections in the water, one of them always stills, becomes perfectly clear on the surface. The thing that baffles me completely, that troubles me, is the fact that I can be a woman who prays for strangers but remains completely blind to their bruises.

A KNOCK ON THE DOOR

**If you find it in your heart to care for
somebody else, you will have succeeded.**

—MAYA ANGELOU

I HAVE BEEN ROUGHING IT IN AN HISTORIC HOTEL IN TEXAS. Sometimes writers have to pay a high price for being on the road. Actually, this wonderful place is pretty cushy, and there is a claw-foot tub in the bathroom where I have tried to take three baths a day just to appreciate it. The only challenging factor here are the narrow, steep, winding staircases that lead to my room.

It's a great place to write, an incredible little picturesque town that makes me want to hole up in this room writing for at least a month. No, I don't always get so cozy, comfortable. But I'm appreciating it while I can. I was just in Jackson, Mississippi, where I met with the Pulpwood Queens book club, and crossed through Louisiana bayou country to Texas for two more nights of discussion about books and the written word. During the process and along the way, I am meeting people, praying for strangers, and picking up stories. But none more than the stories I end up gathering from today's special person that came my way and just cracked me up in the best way possible. It began with a knock on the door. Where it will end up, I'm not yet sure.

The knock was a *blam, blam* kind of knock. "Housekeeping," a voice calls.

I'm parked in a chaise lounge chair, legs up, coffee by my side, and MacBook in my lap, typing away. "C'mon in," I yell in a very Southern fashionable kind of way, which means about as loud as I can.

No one answers and no one comes in. I put the laptop down and get up and open the door. Joline—so her name tag reads—is standing there in a white uniform staring at me.

"Hey," I tell her. "C'mon in."

Now, I am better at cleaning up any hotel room I ever stay in than I am my own house. My grandmother was a housekeeper for a beach hotel when I was a teenager and there must be some residual awareness of this floating in my bones. Perhaps images of rooms that had been vacated by the spring break "children" and the mess that they would leave behind. Regardless of the reason, I'm pretty tidy about the bed, picking up, putting things where they belong.

Now, I sit back down on the lounger and put the laptop back on my lap but I'm watching Joline, who has walked into the room with her hands on her hips and a little bit of "born with it" attitude. On top of that, I get a feeling her back might be hurting just a degree.

"No need to change the sheets," I tell her. "I barely moved. They're all right." It's true, my mind may toss and turn, but I can wake up the same way I lie down.

She surveys the room, looks over my head at the bathroom door behind me, and asks, "You gonna need towels?"

I hate to put her out, but that's the one thing I would like. "Oh, yes, ma'am, extra towels would be great." I intend to read an entire novel in that claw foot before I check out of here. "But everything else is good."

I look at Joline again and I know she's my stranger, but I don't say anything right away. First, I'm thinking about her age—she's probably a good few years older than I am and I'm thinking about her carrying sheets and towels and dirty linens up and down those winding stairs, so I say, "Honey, you need to be careful on those stairs."

She looks at me and says, "Who you think you tellin' to be careful? You think you got to tell me to be careful? I done fell up 'em and I fell down 'em, too. You don't need to tell me about them stairs." Then she sat down on the edge of the bed and went on to tell me a few other things. I stopped writing, put the laptop down, and stood up out of respect to listen. Not that one must stand to be respectful but at the moment that's what felt right. Joline told me about being hurt, about going to the doctor, about having to take medi-

cine. Then she went on to tell me she couldn't keep on taking that medicine because it caused her to just lay up in the
bed all day. She told me about her son and her neighbors
and all the troubles they face.

By the time she finished all that, what I wanted to say
was—*Joline, let me help you clean those last few rooms and we'll get a
cooler full of whatever you want cold to drink and go sit down by the river
and tell stories for the rest of the day.* But I had a deadline and so did
Joline, so we went on about our business. But I did tell her
before she left that I had this little thing I did every day and
that she was my special person. Then I gave her a hug. I'm
proud to say she hugged me back.

After Joline left, I went back to writing. But my mind
drifted, thinking about Joline, her injury, and all those she
holds near and dear. She's clearly a lady who works hard
because she has to. And I think about myself, my writing. I
hear piano music drift up from the lobby and I think about
being here, in this grand hotel, with a claw-foot tub. And I
get back to work, because who can't write something in a
fine hotel with wafting notes of a baby grand finding their
way up those winding stairs?

A Perfect Girl

I do believe we're all connected. I do believe in
positive energy. I do believe in the power of prayer. I
do believe in putting good out into the world. And I
believe in taking care of each other.

—HARVEY FIERSTEIN

SHE'S BEAUTIFUL, TO BE CERTAIN, BUT IT'S NOT THE CLOTHES
she wears, it's her style, the way she wears them, that
makes her stand out in a crowd. She has that certain sort
of panache that some women have at five or eighty-five for
dressing up or down, mixing colors, accessorizing. I admire
it but don't understand it. To me, accessory means pick up
your black purse that matches your black turtleneck which
wears well over jeans. If I'm really being fashionable, the
turtleneck will be white.

I'm at the Thai restaurant in town where the pad Thai
is a popular choice. I'm eating alone with a good novel for
company and loving every minute of it, in spite of the noise

of the full dining room at this busy lunchtime spot. I glance at the girl on line and go back to the words on the page. All is quiet and well in my self-contained space within the crowd. Then I look up and see the girl is getting her food. Next time I glance up, she's sitting alone at the table. Here's where you can insert the heavy sigh. I really don't want to speak to her, or to interrupt my private lunch. I go back to eating and reading, look up in a few minutes, and notice her again. I particularly don't want to interrupt my lunch for Little Miss Perfection. She walks pretty, picks up her utensils pretty, looks like the cover-of-a-magazine-in-spring pretty.

Finally, I'm thinking I'll just get this over with so I can get back to my own little world. I turn my book over and walk my unstylish writer self over to the girl. Next thing you know I'm leaning down in front of her and telling her my same old story and asking her name.

"Trisha," she says. "And it is so funny that you picked me for your stranger."

This is when I want to tell her that I'm not sure I really pick anyone and that, if I did, I wouldn't pick her. I'd always pick the homeless people, or someone who at least looks like they are in need of prayer. Trisha is young, beautiful, wearing killer shoes and a scarf. She's not exactly a "*please pray for me today*" poster child.

"Really?" I put my head on my hand and wait for this story. She's even pretty when she's perplexed.

"Yes, I'm actually going out today to job hunt. I'm just

knocking on doors today looking for a job. I'm pretty nervous about it."

I've hated job hunting all of my life. Maybe everyone does, but it wears on me. It's the paperwork, the application, ascribing things to certain dates and years. I've never been asked a bonus question that inquired something like, "What's the best production of Beckett's *Endgame* you've ever seen?" Or "What was playwright Horton Foote really like in person?" These things I could answer easily, but the applications always ask for those things that escape me— the general applicable facts. Where were you working most recently? And for how long exactly and what did you do there? And whom can we contact now from that place of business? *Are you serious? What kind of test is this? Can't you just read my résumé?* My entire application says, *See My Résumé. There's lots of experience in there. Lots and lots of different kinds of experience. Which all lead to some really good stories, by the way.*

I've never gotten a job that really required a great chronological résumé. I just haven't had a chronological life.

I look at Trisha in her high heels and stylish clothes and I don't envy her a bit. *I want to say, Look, Trisha—all they care about are the dates. Trust this gypsy writer soul who has a mosaic for a résumé, a year of working as the director of a nonprofit in the mountains of Mexico, a year in another state as a case manager, seven months on contract for a community vision campaign, and so it goes on and on forever. Odd jobs, contract writing jobs, grant writing jobs. What the eagle-eyed personnel director may view as a deficiency, I simply see as my life. I can tell someone about early mornings filled with hot-air balloons, chamisa blooming on the mesa, the smell of green chilies in the air, but the logical sequence of events that delivered those experiences into my life? There aren't any. I end up daydreaming about those characters who walked into my case managing office, all beautiful souls who needed help in the worst way, or the soft, pastel sunrises in the rain forests of Costa Rica, but the chronological, exact dates of my last ten years of employment? My brain never ever saw a reason to attempt to capture that. It's hopeless, Trisha, I want to say.* But instead I say, "Well, if it's any consolation, you don't look nervous. You look beautiful." And I mean that. I no longer think of her as Little Miss Perfection; now I see her like one of my best friends' daughters whom I adore. I'd say it from my heart without feeling the least bit snarky about it.

"Oh, thanks so much."

Then we talk about her life, about her personal life and the things that have led her to today and this job-hunting point. About the kind of work she's looking for and what she'd really like to do. Eventually, I ready to leave her to her lunch and get back to my reading.

"Thanks again, this really helps today. I'll feel much better about everything, you know."

I do know. If someone had been praying for me, or told me that they were praying for me, I would have appreciated that on application day. Maybe I would have remembered a few dates and places. But Trisha teaches me something more important.

That the beautiful, yes, they, too, have their stories and

they're not all glory. That even those wearing designer shoes need prayer. I'd like to think they don't, but how spiritually shortsighted of me. How terribly prejudiced for me to perceive someone this way. But I'm learning. Thanks to the Trishas in the world, I'm learning.

THE FACE OF LOSS

**Prayer is not eloquence, but earnestness; not the
definition of helplessness, but the feeling of it; not
figures of speech, but earnestness of soul.**

—HANNAH MORE

TODAY I SEE MY YOUNGEST SON OFF ON A PLANE THAT WILL carry him to Iraq. I am not in the mood to pray for a stranger. Strangers are not really the closest thing to my heart at the moment. My son is. And what I want is for strangers to be praying for these young men and women who are risking their lives in dedication to the oath that they have taken to serve this country in times of war and peace. I want people to pray for peace for the world . . . or at least to pray for the peace of a mother who is not very happy this morning—me. It is a cloudless, sunny day in Nashville, one where I should be simply happy to be alive, but instead I am in real need of prayer myself because I'm not doing so well.

Okay, I'm worse that that. I'm a wreck. I was a major

wreck all day yesterday, calling my son every few hours to say inane things like, "What are you doing now?" and "Do you want to go out to dinner?" and "Do you want me to bake you cookies?" It's a wonder I wasn't trying to chase him down with cherry PEZ candy all night as he packed, as if me forcing childhood things on him would return him to the safety of being my child.

So I barely survived the night, sleeping fitfully, but now I've put on the best face I can to see him off. I shed a few tears, but I don't throw myself around his feet, clinging and screaming, "Don't go!" What I'm thinking about as I see him off in his uniform are all the little plucked wildflowers and weeds, roots and dirt still clinging, that he brought home to me clutched in his tight little fist. This talented practical joker, this *baby* of mine, on his way to potentially witness terrors that I've tried to protect him from all my life. Praying for strangers? I've had some great experiences so far praying for people, but it's better for them if they are not depending on me today. It's better if nobody is depending on me today.

I pick up the morning paper and throw it in the car as I'm leaving to drive to the airport. A few hours and many tears later, I finally open the paper and there she is. In a retrospective of Nashville's previous year. My stranger. It's a face of devastation, weeping over the ruins of what was once her home and all that she owned eaten by the devastating tornados that had assailed us. Her face is my fear. The face of what I would look like if my son doesn't make it back home. It's the face of a history erased and not to be replaced. I'm stricken by the rawness of it. I'm almost wounded by its open honesty of loss and pain and amazed that the paper has printed the photo. I suppose it was newsworthy, this capturing the moment, but it's much too personal and too honest to be printed. I know what this feels like. My house burned to the ground when I was five. Nothing was saved. The rattled displacement in my soul is still there all these years later. Having life and precious pieces erased in a few hours is something I still remember like it was yesterday.

I tear out the article. In spite of my state, my fear, my grief, I pray for this person throughout the day, and as I do, it forces me to be pulled out of my own sadness. My fear of a possible future where my son can't bring me flowers anymore is strangely replaced by a real concern for this brown-eyed woman.

I search for the name of the town the woman lived in. I call Information to find her phone number. I want to tell her that someone is thinking of her, and I hope in the months that have passed since the picture was first taken that she has been able to begin to rebuild her life, or at least to find a little peace and a place of rest. A lady at the newspaper was able to tell me her name, but when I call Information in the town mentioned in the article, she isn't listed. I check the surrounding cities, but no luck. Maybe she has moved on, or moved in with friends. I'm unable to locate her. I put the phone down and I have to remind myself that my purpose isn't to find her, or to even offer her the fifty dollars I would like to give toward the project of rebuilding her life. My purpose is to pray for her. The act of doing this, of actually giving concentrated effort to do this, reminds me that I trust in this weird, invisible thing we call prayer. And as I do that, I have to remind myself if I trust in prayer for a stranger, for a life rebuilt, then surely I can try my best to trust in prayers for the safety of my sons.

Trying my best looks a little ragged round the edges. I just keep hearing that old song, "Standing on Shaky Ground." My prayers feel like that right now. Weak, scattered words over shaky ground. But the image of this woman, kneeling on ground ripped clean of all her promises, has helped me make it through this day. In a way she will never know, she has stabilized me, forced me out of my panicked state and into one where caring for someone unknown made me a better human being. I don't just say a prayer for her, I whisper a thank-you to that woman in the picture before I fold it and put it away. This is the way it is going, these strangers that either know, or will never know, that I am lifting them up, offering them the smallest benediction. They are invading my life in the most precious way. They are rescuing me from a numb life, cut off from the rest of the world because I'm preoccupied by my own pressing needs. They are rescuing me from my indifference.

A MOTHER'S LOVE

I remember my mother's prayers and they have always followed me. They have clung to me all my life.

—ABRAHAM LINCOLN

I'VE ALWAYS TALKED TO GOD. I GREW UP AT THE KNEES OF A grandmother who prayed, and it filtered down into the essence of my life. What I've never fully captured is that prayer could be more than a vertical connection to God. It never really occurred to me that it could be a connection to other people. Now, every day I delve deeper into people's stories, and my heart feels like it's been turned inside out. It would have been easier never telling anyone what I was up to. But the lady in the bus station showed me how much it might mean to tell someone I'm praying for them, so I try to do that. Not every day, but most days. I walk through crowds knowing that someone will stand out to me in a special way. It makes me notice people differently than I ever have. I mean really notice them. I used to be a little more removed from the human race, unplugged, and unmoved. I was just moving through my day and it was so simple. Now, I'm watching everyone.

It's been raining all day in Nashville and I do mean all day. And it's the kind of day where I have more errands to run than I have time in my pocket. I'm under a deadline, which for a writer means words on the paper or editing to be done. But in the meantime I have to shop for lots of things in multiple stores, and I don't like it. It's interfering with my deadline, and by nature I'm not a good shopper anyway, which doesn't make the going any easier. As a matter of fact, it makes me a little grumpy. I'm beginning to see why my daddy used to be the champion of buying things from TV ads. No fuss, no muss—just pick up the phone and buy. Instead, I'm parking, driving, loading and unloading—and wet.

Somewhere in the back of my mind is the thought that I need to be praying for someone, but I really don't have time for it. Instead I'm thinking I need new shoes for a special event and I'm running late. Late, I tell you, and I'm hosting a small dinner party at our house and I haven't started cooking and it's getting later and . . . as I start walking out the door of a store, a young woman is walking in at the same time. I know she's my special someone as if I've been hit by a bolt of lightning. Okay—a small bolt, but it's unmistakable. I don't always choose people by some strange spiritual gut instinct. Sometimes it's just the old man push-

ing my grocery cart to the car or the kid making my sandwich, but today—in my "hurry, rush, try to get it all done"
life—it's the girl walking in as I'm walking out. Wouldn't
you just know it? An added inconvenience. I'm already out
of the store and back into the rain, but there is no denying
that feeling that for some reason this particular person I'm
passing needs to be told that she gets today's lottery prayer
ticket of the day.

I've had my share of bad days—days when nothing goes
right, when I wished I had never gotten out of bed, when I
wished for a different life. Oh, I know that everyone has burdens to bear, and there's no such thing as a perfect life, but
dang, some days are just so hard, and at the very least I wish
there was someone to reassure me and tell me everything is
going to be all right.

There was a long, stressful day at work followed by me
rushing to pick little boys up from after-school care, followed by a pizza run. The pizza run was planned to be our
saving grace. We'd kick off our shoes, have slices of pepperoni with extra cheese, a Coke, and a smile over home-
work before bedtime. Only it didn't go that way. Instead I
found that I had grabbed the wrong keys in the morning
and locked us out of the house. It was dark, it was a school
night, and as we stood there with me trying to figure out
what to do next, it started to rain. Seriously. Not a bad day,
just a major inconvenience.

I've lived through frozen pipes, hurricanes, sick children,

tornados, floods, and facing down the great unknown. I pressed on but sometimes the road got more than a little rough and rocky.

One of the rockiest of them was the day that I had juggled to get both sons off to school, taken leave from work, and rushed into the hospital just before my father had a triple heart bypass. This was back in the days when people of various professions wore pagers. When my pager went off during my father's surgery for me to call my son's school, I knew it wouldn't be good. Turned out it wasn't. My son had gotten into trouble recently and any call from the school meant a black cloud on the horizon was growing wider. My concern for my son, his influences, and his direction was growing by huge degrees. So was my concern for my father to make it out of the hospital.

I waited until I knew Dad was safely out of surgery before I took that lonely ride down the elevator, walked to my car, and drove tearfully to my son's school to meet with the principal.

Now, I look back at that day in the midst of what I'm doing by speaking to others, speaking to strangers and being determined to continue this journey with something that sometimes borders happy determination and sometimes introverted desperation, and I think, *What if?*

What if on that particular day, after I'd had that pager go off followed by a terse conversation with the school, and looked at my father's ashen face as he was wheeled to the recovery room—what if a stranger had stepped onto that elevator and said the words that I've now said so many times, "Today, you stood out to me and I'll be saying special prayers and blessings for you."

On that day if anyone had asked me if there was anything special I needed, I would have started crying. Or I would have at least swallowed hard and tried to mention my dad's and son's situations. Okay, in doing that, I would have started crying. One thing is for certain—that person would have had no doubt that when they ran into me, I was indeed their stranger of the day. I could've used a special stranger's prayer that day.

Years earlier, when I was still a teenager, I came home to discover that my mother had been in a horrible car accident. I couldn't even drive yet and called a taxi to get to the hospital. I don't remember the first thing about the ride there. Not what the driver looked like, the color of his hair, or the roads he turned down. What I do remember is sitting and crying alone outside the waiting room, as my mother was still in intensive care.

Three women across the family waiting room whispered behind their hands to one another as they furtively continued to glance my way. My mother was in a very bad way, near death, and obviously the news had traveled the floor. Suddenly a different woman approached me. "Is that your mother in there?" she asked. I guess no other details were necessary as I nodded and wiped my sodden face. She walked away and in a short amount of time reappeared, opened a new box of tissues, and passed them to me. Then she patted me on the shoulder, leaned over, and whispered, "Don't worry now. Your mother is going to be all right."

An angel? No, I don't think so. I think it was just a stranger who had decided the bubble of her world could be broken. That she could cross that crazy, invisible line that seems to hold us back, separate us from one another. In looking back on that moment, there is no question in my mind that the other three women, glancing and whispering behind their hands, were equally sorry for me but they chose to stay in the safety of their private worlds.

These memories remind me that sometimes a simple word, a gentle touch, is worth the trouble. That moving out of the skin of my comfort zone is worth the momentary risk.

I turn around and reenter the store and say, "Excuse me," and interrupt her life. The same way my life has continued to be interrupted every day now for days on end. The same way I continue to interrupt others with "Excuse me but I have this resolution," "Excuse me but may I ask your name," "Excuse me but I have to detain you." This is the way life is developing for me now. On a daily basis I'm approaching strangers and saying, "Excuse me." It hasn't gotten any easier because it's always an inconvenience for both of us— me and the person I speak to. Who stops or slows down anymore to talk to a stranger in this crazy, busy world we live in? It's a good thing I live in the South, where people are more accustomed to being talked to by well-meaning people on the street.

"Excuse me, but I made this resolution at the beginning of the year . . ." and so I begin. I can see her take a deep breath, most likely trying to rescue her patience, trying to listen to somebody's story as she waits. Then her eyes widen as I keep speaking, and she smiles.

"You don't know how much that means to me!" She puts her hand over her heart. "My mother passed away from breast cancer a few months ago, and I just miss her so much and . . ." Now she has tears in her eyes and I notice she's wearing a Breast Cancer Awareness T-shirt. Obviously, a shirt she wears frequently, a reminder and a challenge to those who can see it. A way for her to fight for her mother even though her mother is gone.

When a mother sees a girl who has lost her mother and misses her on the verge of breaking down, you know what that person needs: a mother's hug. And she gets one from me. I step up and hug her, saying, "Everything's going to be all right." Then she tells me that I have made her day and she leaves wearing a brand-new smile. It doesn't matter if I ever hear from her or see her again, although I really wish I could. I know that on this day we did what people need to do more often—we connected. I never realized until now, until this year and this thing I'm doing, how much a word might mean to someone. A word that just comes out of the blue from someone who doesn't know them. I'm beginning to learn that this resolution is no ordinary thing. All the busy body, wet errands I was running suddenly took a backseat to one girl missing her mama and getting the hug she needed to help her make it through her day.

STREET CORNER CONNECTIONS

**Our prayers must mean something to us if they are to
mean anything to God.**

—MALTBIE D. BABCOCK

SOMETIMES YOU MEET PEOPLE WHO EXHIBIT MORE ENERGY, joy, and life in five minutes than the rest of us do in a lifetime. My Uncle John was like that. He was the kind of man who was captivated by the smell that comes just before or after a summer rain, by the greenness of ripe avocados, and by all the beauty of a given day. He was the one that took me outside saying, "You just can't miss this!" to watch a heat-lightning storm on the horizon.

It's a rainy Monday morning in Nashville, and I'm on the wrong street. I'm trying to see between the rain, have missed my turn on a one-way street, and am now driving in the opposite direction than I need to be going. With the rain and the traffic, I'm having a difficult time trying to find a good place to turn around and go back the way I came when the man in the parking garage smiles and motions for me to turn in. He's wearing this big Monday morning smile, reminding me of my uncle. He motions me forward again and I pull into the garage and roll the window down.

"Hey, I'm just trying to turn around," I yell out the window.

"Well, you better be careful so you don't get in an accident. Don't back out, turn around here." He is all baggy pants, big smile, white hair.

"What's your name?"

"Lucca!" He throws both of his arms in the air to punctuate the wonderfulness of his name.

"Look, I have this resolution . . ."

"To go out and find a man named Lucca." He throws both arms in the air again.

"No, it's not that, it's that I have this . . ." I am laughing and trying to work my way to the resolution, to tell him that he is my stranger, but now there are cars behind me trying to get into the garage and they are honking.

"I've gotta go. Thanks, Lucca." I begin driving through figuring, you know, I'll just pray for him. That's all there is to it. I've got a busy day ahead and I'm trying to make it to a special meeting downtown.

I believe sometimes that there are encounters so divinely

timed that *not believing* in some sort of universal travel agent angel in charge of divine encounters with impeccable timing would be the most bizarre thing. A few years ago I had traveled to New York for both business and pleasure. One early evening I had plans to meet fellow authors who lived in the city at the Algonquin Hotel. My only problem was I got off the bus blocks away from my destination. Then I did what maybe most people in New York City don't do—I chose a stranger from the crowd and asked directions. It was a man standing on the corner just kind of looking around. I guess, for one thing, he wasn't walking by at a lightning pace so he was much easier to approach. I said my usual "I'm lost, please help me, and do you know the way to this hotel?" The man looked at me thoughtfully, considered the Algonquin, and sent me off in at least what we both hoped was the right direction. A few days later I received an e-mail from this man. That's right. An e-mail. He told me that he just couldn't believe that at that exact time of day, the author River Jordan had approached him on a corner in New York, but then he checked my website, read my blog, and saw that indeed it was me. The man lived in Tennessee and had attended a book signing of mine in Nashville. He and his wife happened to be vacationing for an impromptu weekend. She had stepped into a salon to have her nails done. He waited a little while and decided to step outside and just simply stand on the corner and look around. Then I arrived at that exact moment to inquire about directions. Millions of people in the city, on the streets, passing corners. Millions of exact moments intersecting and there I was like some wild character popping up from a book asking for the yellow brick road.

So this sort of strange "travel agent of the universe" thought arises when six months after I meet this Lucca, I look up and there he is again. Out of the blue, walking across a parking garage. This time, though, he's not so high-stepping.

"Hey, Lucca, how's it going?" It's a good question to ask because today he seems to be a little lackluster, missing a whole lot of bravado.

"You know my name?" He stops walking, turns back toward me.

"Oh yes. You helped me turn around one day, to pull out of traffic." I point a finger toward him. "You set me on due course. And you don't know it but you were my stranger that day."

"*I* was your stranger? Me?" He points to his chest, making certain I meant him as if I were talking to fifty people. We are currently alone in the garage. It's getting later and the light is fading fast.

"Yes, you were. I pray for a different stranger every day and that day—you were my stranger."

"You prayed for me?" He gets a serious look in his eye and, a hushed, almost kind of reverent tone to his voice.

"Well, you didn't know it, but I sure did."

He puts his hands in his pants pockets, stands there looking somewhere over my head and considering. "I'm going to go home and think about this."

"Well, all right. Have a good day Lucca."

"Oh, I'll have a better day now." Then I go my way and he goes his. I might never bump into him again but this one time was enough because sometimes people need to know, need to be told that they stood out in a special way to someone. That they can travel through three airports and multiple time zones, cross cities, and geographical borders and still wind up at the exact spot they need to be to hear the message meant for them.

In Lucca's case, I'm thinking this was the day he needed to hear it most. And there I was walking through the garage at the same time he was. It's not just a simple coincidence.

In Sickness and
in Health

But now I am past all comforts here but prayers.

—**SHAKESPEARE,** *HENRY VIII*

FOR MONTHS I'VE BEEN PRAYING FOR THE SICK. IF NOT THE person that I introduce myself to, then often it's for their mother, daughter, son, or husband. The list is long, the needs are great. Everyone I meet seems to have a great need for a touch of that old balm of Gilead. But now it's my husband who is sick and is in the emergency room. He's been hit with a horrible monster bag full of symptoms. I was so worried about his fever and him being dehydrated that I finally badgered him into seeing a doctor, and of course, it's the weekend so our only option is the emergency room. As a testament to how sick he really is, I have actually managed to get him in the car and to weakly agree to this extravagance. This is a man who has taped up his

own concussion with duct tape so he can keep working. I
kid you not.

Now we are jumping through all the hoops of the emergency waiting room ritual. We have finally been called into
triage. The nurse is soft-spoken and kind. She is very gentle
with him (which, for the record, was not the tone I was
using to get him in the car). I know he is certainly not her
first patient of the day. She's been at this for a long shift and
the waiting room is packed. Her day is overflowing with
worried and pained faces.

I'm listening to that soft voice, watching the calm way
she touches my husband, assures him that she understands,
and I know she is the person I'm to pray for today. But she is
doing her job, which is to take care of my husband and not
to have someone say, "Oh, guess what? I have this resolution and . . ." The worry that I have over troubling people,
of interrupting their lives, or appearing a little crazy in the
process, has not gone away. Somehow I manage to trudge
on through this scenario day after day in spite of myself and
all my misgivings about what people will think of me.

My husband is shaking with chills and actually moaning
from pain, and here I am thinking about praying for this
woman and whether or not I should tell her. Also, I think
about the entire scenario and wonder about how this whole
prayer resolution announcement will be received. People
sick everywhere and I'm telling the nurse that I'm praying
for *her*? I feel as if I'm some warped version of Dorothy and

Toto asking to see the wizard. I am continually paranoid, and yet I push on, although I don't say anything quite yet.

We are processed and sent to a room to wait for the doctor. I pace a little as my husband groans and lies down on the bed. I keep peeking out the door for signs of the nurse. Don't think I'm not sensitive to the husband there. Yes, I am praying for him, too, but right now I know I have to talk to the nurse in triage. I open the door again and peek out. There she is. She's standing at the edge of another door. I motion for her to come to me. "I can't move. I'm watching a patient. You have to come to me." I tell my sick husband I'll be right back. Now, the most wonderful thing about my man at this moment is he understands. He thought the resolution was a great idea and he has become used to me saying, "Just one moment," and then walking off into a crowd to have a word with someone.

I approach the nurse and tell her the same thing I tell everyone. Today you're my special stranger to pray for. I have the realization that we are surrounded by sick people, everyone here seemingly needs prayer, yet it's this woman who looks well, who is caring for others, that has my undivided attention. And instead of pointing out this kind of absurdity to me, she gets a funny look in her eyes and a smile on her face. "Thank you, *so much*," she says.

I start to walk away, turn back, and say, "No problem, really. I just wanted you to know."

"But wait," she calls after me. I go back and stand beside

her. "My husband just had open-heart surgery," she says, and then she leaves a lot of words unsaid and says so much more with tears in her eyes.

"So it's been a tough season for you."

"Yes," she replies, "it's been a tough season." And she thanks me a few more times even though it's not necessary. It's never necessary. It's enough for me to know, to really know, that strangers need prayers. And that the strangers laid on my heart need them sometimes most of all on that given day.

What I am learning is that when I pray for strangers I fully expect those prayers, in all their detached third-party, innocent bystander, agendalessness—to be answered. I actually *feel* them being answered. The faith attached to these prayers is tangible, it's different when I pray for my children, my family, and my husband. When I pray for those closest to me, it almost feels selfish. I pray for my own family out of my need for that love to continue. For them to be well and stay well, safe, and happy, because truly—all codependent counseling aside—for this woman raised in the South in the midst of the multitudes, their happiness is linked to my happiness. So I know that there is a very selfish need on my part to have those prayers answered. I want what I perceive my children and family and friends need to happen in their lives. Unfortunately my prayers become like old delivery lists where people could call the corner grocery or drugstore, place their order, and have it delivered that day. Lovely concept. And that's exactly how my prayers fall toward my family. Checklist prayers for security, safety, love, jobs, happiness, peace, and prosperity of the best kind, for the successes in their lives that matter most.

But praying for Sharon? Praying for her to have strength in this season as she battles fear and exhaustion, cares for people all day, and goes home to take care of her husband after serious surgery. It's not very selfish. What difference is it really going to make in my life if Sharon's burden is lightened or her husband survives? That would be an eternal question, but I'm thinking it matters a lot more than I am aware. I am thinking that our lives will be traced back to the moments where we were selfless. Where we took time to offer a kind word or a listening ear. I'm just thinking that someday it's all going to matter very much.

THE FLU BLUES

I believe in prayer. It's the best way we have
to draw strength from heaven.

—JOSEPHINE BAKER

BEING OPEN EVERY DAY TO A NEW STRANGER WAITING IN the wings isn't always easy, but usually they just show up. I turn the corner and they come into view from a distance and I know—this is *the one*. I can't explain it to anyone. In spite of all the positive aspects of this resolution in my life, I still have to really work to pull myself out of my own life, my worries, and my deadlines. To say my doing this is making me a better person would be an overstatement. If anything, it's showing me exactly who I am. And who I'm not.

The whole experience is like a big push and a wink from heaven that says, "Go on and step out there, you antisocial writer girl. You worried mom, frazzled wife, and deadline-driven whozit—make someone else your priority once a day. Make it someone you don't know and will potentially never see again. Let me see you stretch."

Some days I stretch better than others. Some days my stretcher is broken.

Some days I'm just a worthless lump of clay tossing up prayers to God like dirtballs. Today is a dirtball day. I don't feel good. I am not even going to pray for anyone today. That's what I've decided. Resolutions are meant to be broken. I'm sick with some sort of flu. I feel as if a gorilla has jumped on my body and beaten me up. My skin hurts. My plan is to just take a good-riddance hooky day from my prayer resolution thingy. What's going to change, after all, if I don't pray for a stranger for one day? The world isn't going to shatter and come to an end. Who wants some germ-ridden, feverish maniac praying for them anyway? My only problem is, I have to drive to the store to get that achy-all-over, sniffly, sneezy medicine. Well, one thing is for sure—I'm not talking to anyone, or even looking at anyone. At all. Get the stuff and check out at the self-check so I don't even have to talk to a cashier. That's what I'm doing when I remember I also need something way across the store in the dairy section. So I trudge, mumbling to myself about the old days and how people went to the store only once in a blue moon instead of three times a week.

And then I see a woman in an aisle who catches my eye. Oh great. Now I feel that familiar tug, but I'm determined to ignore it. Today I am my own special stranger, that's the way I'm feeling. I close the door to the dairy case and turn around, and before I know it, I have asked the woman her name.

"Margaret," she says.

In the grumpiest, most unenthusiastic voice you can imagine, I say, "Margaret, look—every day I pray for a stranger that crosses my path, and today you're my special stranger."

Margaret takes three full steps backward when I say this. She stares at me and takes in a deep breath, as her eyes fill with tears. Then she rushes forward, grabs me, and hugs me tightly, all the while saying, "Thank you, thank you, thank you!" She won't let me go and she repeats it over and over nonstop. I try to take a step back, to at least protect her from whatever cootie germs I'm carrying and ask her if there is anything special she wants me to pray for. "For everything," she says. "For absolutely everything. For my family." Then Margaret's daughter, who is shopping with her and has heard and witnessed all of this, thanks me, too. She passes me after her mother finally walks on and tells me again, "Thank you, again. Thank you so much. You just don't know what that means."

I think, *Prayer isn't just this thing reserved for Sundays,* and it's not just for, "Now I lay me down to sleep," or saying grace over the annual Thanksgiving meal. It is perhaps one of the greatest human connectors in this world. A chain that runs from one carbon life-form to another, an unseen force that makes a strong vertical leap into the mysteries of the unknown. The place where prayers travel to and where they might be captured, opened, and answered.

I'm moved to come out of my self-focused, playing-hooky, feel-bad hiding. I'm moved to earnestly pray for Margaret, to lift her up and speak blessings into her life silently to myself as I watch her and her daughter walk away. It really isn't much too much to ask, is it? A moment to pray silently in my heart. To really slow down and to compassionately offer up a cup of prayer for a stranger. I do believe in miracles. I do believe that the darkest tide can take an unexpected turn in another direction. I believe life is meant to be fulfilled, purposes completed, and that the people who cross our paths all have something to teach us, if we'll only take just the moment to stop and listen. Margaret has taught me that sick or well, tired or not, my prayers can make a difference to someone. I guess I'll save that hooky card for other things like mopping floors and doing laundry.

SIMPLE PRAYERS

Prayer is not an old woman's idle amusement.
Properly understood and applied, it is the
most potent instrument of action.

—MAHATMA GANDHI

A LOT OF PEOPLE LOVE TO QUOTE NIETZSCHE'S FAMOUS SAYing, "What doesn't kill me makes me stronger." I've come to believe something a little different, namely, that life can give you a total knockout and that what doesn't kill you might make you wish you were dead. It's why the word *suicide* is in our vocabulary. People really do reach a place where going on just doesn't seem like an option.

There's a woman in the grocery aisle next to me who looks like she might be at the end of her rope. She looks tired and rough. Like life has knocked her to the mat and she's having a hard time getting up. I once met someone who looked a lot like her. The details surrounding our first meeting came about in such a way that she thought I had passed right through some ethereal cloud and landed on her doorstep. She actually believed I was an angel. She had her reasons, considering the circumstances. She had been seriously planning her suicide minutes before we met, when she thought she'd toss up one last prayer in the process, something to this effect: "Lord, if you want me to live and not die today, just send someone to my door that will just listen to my story." A simple request. Before she could get up off her knees from the floor, she heard the sound of my car pulling up in the empty driveway. True story.

I happened to be driving around a neighborhood and saw a For Sale sign in the yard of a house. I wasn't looking for a house to buy, but it occurred to me that for no reason at all I should take a look just in case I should run into someone who was house hunting and needed a tip about this place. There was no car in the driveway and the house appeared vacant, so I pulled up and parked. I got out of the car and started trying to peek through the front door glass when the door suddenly flew open. The woman was standing there staring at me with a wild look in her eyes. She invited me in to look at the house but then she turned to me and said something like, "Could you possibly take time to hear my story?" Well, I'll be truthful, I couldn't—I had to go to the dry cleaners, pick up a few things from the grocery store, and go home to prepare dinner; I didn't have time to stop and listen. But I did anyway, never realizing she had just been thinking of checking out on life.

She took her story from the top, or maybe the middle—it doesn't really matter. She'd had a few hard knocks, life had gotten tough, and one bad event had led to a long chain of occurrences that ran from bad to worse. Regardless, the telling of the story, and the tears that went with those words, seemed to be the medicine she needed, and at the end of my listening spell, she took time to share what she had been praying just as she heard my car drive up. She was crying and hugging me when I left. She no longer had a car, so the next day I boxed up some groceries for her and at the last minute tossed one of my old Bibles in the box. I included a note with my home and work phone numbers. She wasn't at the house when I returned, so I left the box on the doorstep. She called me a few times and life got better for her. In time, she moved back to Virginia to be near her daughter and I heard from her a few more times after that.

Now I'm years and states away, but as I pass this woman in a grocery aisle, I notice that she looks rough, worn, and tired. I've seen this before, I think. I don't mean the kind of rough, worn, and tired that I feel at the end of seemingly every day. I mean, life has been rough. Either today, this week, or forever, things have gone from bad to worse for her. I turn around to ask her name. "Lisa," she says.

I tell her about my resolution business, and that I'll be praying for her. She thanks me. I start to walk away, and then I turn around, walk toward her, and take the time to ask her if there is anything special she'd like prayer for. "Yeah," she says, "I've got my kitchen tore to heck and back." She runs a working woman's hand through her hair. When I say working, I mean that. Hands chapped, rough, and dirty. "I'd appreciate it if you'd pray I get it put together again." I tell her I've been through torn-up kitchens, that I know how that feels, and that I'll pray that her kitchen gets put together. Then I turn to go, but she's still standing there thinking and she adds, "And pray that I have a good life. That's all I ask for," she says, "just a good life."

"Sure 'nuff. Got it. A good life for Lisa." And the feeling I get from Lisa is that by good life, she means just that. A simple life. The basics in life. Shelter, food, and if it's not too much to ask for, love.

It will be months before I see Lisa again. I see her as I'm walking out of the same store and she's walking in with a friend. She downright sparkles, she looks so bright. The very air around her is lighter. I smile at her as I pass. She turns and says, "Hey, don't I know you?"

"Yes," I tell her, "we met in the aisle one night when—" She interrupts me quickly, "That's right, I remember you. I remember." Maybe she doesn't want to be remembered that way or perhaps that whole prayer thing might be embarrassing in front of her friend.

"How's that kitchen coming?"

It's her friend who steps up to answer that question. She whips out a cell phone and approaches me.

"I'll show you how it's coming. Just look at these. It's all finished."

I take time to look at all the photos. To really look at them and appreciate the quality of the work, the color of the tile, the design of the cabinets. The kitchen is beautiful. Truly. Those working woman hands did a great job. She's noticeably happier, and it appears her prayer for a simple, good life is coming to pass. A little place to call one's own, a working kitchen, a friend, a good life filled with simple things. I tell her how beautiful everything looks and to have a nice night. It feels so good to see her smiling.

The more amazing thing to me is not how great Lisa looks or that her life has turned a better corner, but that seeing her this way has made the light in my life a little brighter.

It doesn't seem to take much for some people. All they ask for is for someone to listen, really listen, to their story. Or for just a good life. They're only asking for the basic things. Shelter and someone to love.

I get in my car, roll down the window, and breathe in the night air thankful for the simple pleasures, a warm house, a great friend, a bowl of soup. A good life.

On a Wing and a Prayer

Prayer is nothing else than being on terms of friendship with God.

—SAINT TERESA OF AVILA

PART OF A WRITER'S LIFE IS TRAVEL, AND THE PAST FEW WEEKS I've been logging many miles. My latest novel, *Saints in Limbo*, was recently released, and since then I have made trips to festivals, book signings, and conferences to promote the story of *Saint*'s main character, Velma True.

Months have passed since my resolution began, and I'm still praying for strangers at home and on the road when I'm traveling. And close to my heart, I'm still praying for my sons, and for all those serving in war zones. Today is one of those busy airport days; weather has taken a turn for the stormy worse and flights are being canceled and delayed. I'm exhausted, feeling weary in my bones from being so many days on the road. The chairs at every gate are occupied. Every table in the coffee shop is filled to capacity. I find a clear spot on the floor—thank God for the invention of blue jeans—and park myself on a spot against the wall with my carry-on.

In just a few minutes, a young man in uniform looking just as travel weary as me finds the only empty spot left, which is next to me on the floor. I'm flying home from a recent book festival; he's flying home on leave from Iraq. The two of us have carved out a small space in a busy airport during a long layover. The voices of travelers are everywhere, announcements of more delays, flights being rerouted, pages for people are constant. It's a noisy spot, but here we are, amid all the chaos, in a little pocket of our own making small talk. For the young man in uniform, this particular trip home is very special. He is seeing his newborn daughter for the first time.

I want to tell him, *You, son, are too young to be a daddy. You're just a baby yourself.* But that's just my mama heart. He's actually a sharp, dedicated young man following his orders of the day. Is it okay that I tremble a little inside? Is it okay when he tells me how worried his mother has been, how she wouldn't miss driving all night up the coast to be there when he arrived, that it brings tears to my eyes? I swallow hard, think baseball, and look away. "I know all about that," I tell him. "I have two sons over there." I keep my eyes averted.

He notices that I've gotten quiet and says a few kind words like, "It's okay. It's really not so bad over there."

I nod and say something stupid like, "Really? Not too bad? Well, that's good."

I talk to him about my sons being in Iraq and Afghanistan and about my daddy being in Vietnam. We talk about wars and mothers and new baby girls. Then Daniel tips his brave hand slightly when he says, "I'm a little worried, though. It's my third trip back. It makes me wonder, you know, about luck."

If I could swipe an angel straight out of heaven at the moment, I would do it. Grab him and place him at Daniel's back and say, "Guard him, wings wide, cover complete." Oh yes, I would. I'd pull down a legion and say, "Guard all the good Daniels of this world. These bright, young, brave, and dedicated people. Guard them beyond anything I can imagine because we need them if this world is to go on. We need these young men and women with their battle-worn faces and polite manners and willingness to defend. The loss of one affects us all, because I've prayed for a mother bent over a flag just placed in her lap and for a dad working head down, sorrow palpable, as the picture of his deceased son hung with honor in the little shop where he worked. That mother's face, that man's body bent with sorrow, this wonderful young man in an airport—they've become my people. And whether or not Daniel makes it home safely to raise that baby girl matters so much to me all I can do is to pray.

REPENTANCE

**One of the secrets in life is that all that is really worth
doing is what we do for others.**

—LEWIS CARROLL

MY MOTHER USED TO SING A SONG WHEN SHE ROCKED ME called "Hang Down Your Head, Tom Dooley," and the rest of the song goes on to say, "poor boy you're bound to die." I don't know why she sang that song except it had a good rhythm for rocking.

I hadn't thought of that song in years or the fact that it was the equivalent of a lullaby for me until I met a young man waiting tables. As is my custom on a pretty regular occasion, I had taken a break from working and gone to lunch alone with the book I was reading at the moment. The young man waiting on me had taken my order, made fresh coffee, and waited on me courteously as I sat there by the window, stoic, reading, and writing. But when he returned one time to refill my cup, I had to say my bit, the whole thing ultimately ending in, "Today you are my stranger."

His reaction was a first for me in my many moons and months of interrupting people's lives with this hello of mine. He hung down his head. Completely, immediately hung down his head as it dropped all the way to his chest. There was a sound that escaped his lips like a sigh or a plaintive noise, a boy in need of confession.

"Hey, Tom," I whispered as I tapped him gently on the back of his right hand, which he had rested on the table. I was a little concerned that he might faint. "It's not a bad thing, you know? It's not like because you did something wrong. It's just a prayer for good things in your life."

He raises his head, looks at me, and swallows hard. He blinks a few times quickly and I tell him my coffee's fine. Everything is good. But I have to be honest; I don't know what's going on between God and Tom or anyone else in his life. Maybe, just maybe, he was in need of some kind of absolution. This isn't a judgment call on my part. I check myself daily on passing judgment and the things that most people would probably judge others for don't move me. I certainly do have my hot buttons, believe me. I get a little angry when I hear that manufacturers are making thongs for seven-year-old girls, that stores are selling them, or that anyone is buying them. Yes, I probably have some judgment issues where those kinds of things are concerned, but the people I meet every day in life, not so much. (Unless they fall into one of the three categories above and then I'd have some things to say.) As for my waiter, Tom? As far as I'm concerned he looks too young to even need some serious forgiveness. What could he have possibly done in all his young life to cause him to hang his head so low, so soon?

As he continues to wait on me, to bring my food, to serve me, I pray that whatever burdens he may carry, even those perhaps self-inflicted, could be lifted. He talks with me a little more at every table visit, asks what I'm reading, I show him the cover and we discuss a few books he's read, and I recommend a few to him because it's what I do, doling out stories like prescriptions. Take a chapter of this one, and forty pages of that one, and call me in the morning.

As I leave, I silently pray that Tom's days will be full of the things he believes in, that the choices he makes will be the ones that make him proud.

Because, really, the memory of one Tom Dooley with his head hung down and getting ready to die is enough for a lifetime. But the world is full of Tom Dooleys, lives lived young and old full of regret and seeking some kind of absolution from old scars or recent sins.

MY HUSBAND HAS a few favorite restaurants in town. All of them local, nonchain-type, neighborhood establishments. This one is casual to say the least, with a menu featuring sandwiches, steaks, and simple fare all offered up in an easy, lazy way. One of our favorites on the menu happens to be some of the best hot wings around. The place is more bar than eatery. There's an open-air dining/drinking area where I prefer to sit, shaded by trees in the summer and away from the televisions showcasing current sports or news.

I've just wrapped the radio show when my husband calls. He's having a late lunch at this place, which happens to be near the station, so I tell him I'll drop by, say hello, and grab a bite to eat. When I arrive, he is sitting where I expect him to be—at the bar, where he swears he gets faster service. My legs kind of dangle from the stool, so I often choose to stand and give my road-warrior, computer-sitting back a break. I order a salad from the congenial bartender and wait. My husband is talking business with an associate, going over flooring samples. I am content to sit quietly, contemplating, working on next week's show or some current novel deadline in my head.

Before the salad can arrive, an old man wanders in, looks across the sea of mostly empty chairs, and chooses the stool right next to me. I manage to stifle a sigh. He looks like trampled, old expectations. Like a person who made a few wrong decisions, a few wrong steps that led off the trail into a leftover life. The kind who finds himself sitting in bars on early afternoons. Killing time until maybe a little serious television show, a police drama with a crime to solve, can lull him into forgetting past mistakes.

He orders a beer and nothing to eat. I try to ignore him

as my salad arrives, and suddenly starving, I dig in. Seven empty stools are to my left yet he has chosen to sit down in the one immediately next to me. I take another bite. I've been talking for two hours solid on the air. My throat feels sore and I really don't want to talk anymore. None of that really matters. I know what's coming soon because I get that feeling in my stomach that this isn't a chance encounter. Soon enough I give in to that familiar tug, put down my fork, and lean toward him.

"What's your name?" I ask him, and so it begins, this personal dance of my confession about what I do, but the tides turn as he begins a confession of his own making.

"John," he says and there is something in this case that moves him. An old man full of regret and questions. And then in a soulful pondering about my resolution—"You do this every day?"

"Pretty much." I search for a business card but don't find one handy. My husband, overhearing, pulls one of mine from his wallet, passes it to me, and continues his own conversation about work with his colleague.

"So, John, I'm a writer and . . ." I'm trying to say almost matter-of-factly—Look, I have a day job, I'm not a priest or some pastor sent out on the missionary fields of bars at large. It's just a thing I do. But it strikes me how being a writer, being published is not more worthy, or more impressive in any way, than me sitting here meeting this man, focusing on his broken life. And yes, it is broken. He alludes to a few things in a low voice, a hushed kind of way, as if I am indeed a priest on the other side of the curtain. Things I'm not sure I understand except for maybe something about his wife, about maybe it's all his fault, and that now he lives alone in a little apartment around the corner. "I have a daughter," he wants me to know, "and she comes to see me."

I know how crazy life can get and how one wrong turn leaves you feeling like Alice, alone and trapped somewhere down the rabbit hole. It does keep me from getting uppity about much.

He's got about three days' growth on his chin. It's not for style. His clothes are rumpled and whatever sleep he's been getting isn't enough to get him by. He's a broken mess of lonely, a man full of regret. A strange, Southern version of Hemingway's character from the story "A Clean, Well-Lighted Place."

"You pray for people like this? I mean, you do this all the time?" he asks me again.

"I do."

"Imagine me coming in here today and finding you. This is important, this thing you're doing. It's a gift, you know, it changes people."

"I don't know anything about that. It's a resolution."

He looks at me bleary-eyed but serious. "See, what I'm saying is, imagine me bumping into you instead of"—he looks around the bar—"well, you know." Then he focuses on my face. "But here I am talking to you about other things. About life and dying and things like God."

I don't speak much. I just listen; interject a word here and there. Then I finish my salad. "Gotta go, John. It's been good meeting you."

He picks my card up off the bar. "You can believe I'm going to keep this. I'm going to remember you, too. I'm going to remember what we talked about."

"And I won't forget you. Trust me on that."

I'm telling the truth. And later that night I pray for John. Now, people have begun to stop and ask me what those prayers look like, what they sound like. "Is it just that you pray for them to have blessings?" Yes. "Do you maybe just envision them, like, in a white light?" Yes, sometimes.

But there are other things, sometimes. There are prayers for a man to find forgiveness and to forgive himself for a life not well lived. There's plenty of room for prayers like that. Just like that old Tom Dooley of the song, we're all bound to die sometime, but I prefer to think it can be with eyes cast upward in hopeful expectation.

Malls and Other Mazes

Prayer only from the mouth is no prayer.

—JAMAICAN PROVERB

I'VE BEEN FORCED TO GO SHOPPING. NOT BY A PERSON, because that generally wouldn't work for me. It's always a speaking engagement, a book festival, signing event, something that has caused me to find something "appropriate" to wear. It leaves me feeling trapped like a mouse in a maze—somewhere at the end there is cheese, surely, one tiny piece of cheese in the form of a new outfit.

What I seem to despise more than going shopping is actually trying on clothes once I arrive at the store. Occasionally, I find someone working in a store that makes the experience at least bearable. My stranger for the day was that person. A smiling college student who ever so patiently offered to bring me sizes large and sizes small. One of those people who had that never-gives-up attitude. As if the next great outfit was always just around the corner but ever so accessible.

My cousin is really, really good at this. She's also a thousand miles away. Sometimes she tries to talk me through
my shopping angst, literally asking me what I need or what
I'm looking for, trying to steer me to the right section in
the right department store while I'm on my cell phone. The
whole experience frustrates me to no end. It tires me to the
bone. I'd rather write another novel. Really.

But I had to go shopping today, and thankfully there
was Cathy, making the experience a bit more bearable. As
she's ringing up my final selections, I have to tell her that
she's my stranger. But instead of focusing on that part, she
asks my name again. When I tell her, she says, "Wait, wait—I
know that name! You're a writer?"

"I am much better at that than I am shopping."

"My mother's book club read one of your books. She
loved it. It's one of her favorites!"

Okay, so my entire shopping experience just became a
touch more cheerful. It was worth the dressing room experience just to hear those words. We talk titles for a minute;
discuss which title her mother just read. Cathy asks when
I'll be at a signing nearby. Regardless of who I might be to
her mother, I haven't forgotten who she is to me.

"Cathy, before I go, do you have anything special that
you'd like me to pray for?"

There's only a slight pause, the answer is right ready on
her tongue. I think it is nice to know the thing that you
would pray for. That maybe it's a good thing to have the

knowledge of it, the thing you seek, want, need, hope for somewhere that you can lay your hand on it.

"My destiny. I'd love to know really, truly, what my purpose in life is."

"An excellent choice," I tell her. Then say my good-byes.

And I do pray later that night for her to find just that, the purpose for her life for this season to be revealed. Because seasons change, life shifts, and new purposes, I believe, can be birthed at any age. I've lived a lot of lives already in one. Put another way, there have been many different chapters in this story of my life, sometimes each seemingly with its own purpose for the season. Ask anyone who knows me. Blame it on the creative spirit, this writer's life, whatever you choose, but I've got stories I could tell you until you are a hundred and two. What I want to say to Cathy is more than she has time to hear between customers. That I will indeed pray for her destiny but that it may not be spot-on for every changing season of her life. My life still changes, and in the middle of being what is most often referred to as a Southern Gothic novelist, I am walking out this resolution and writing the stories down. The unexpected has its place on destiny's trail. Just like meeting Cathy has been, an unexpected pleasure.

NEW FRIENDS

God can pick sense out of a confused prayer.

—RICHARD SIBBES

I'M A STRANGER TO THE PEOPLE I'VE BEEN PRAYING FOR BUT I'M no stranger to prayer. It's been woven into my life in such a way that I have come to believe in its power. On some days those prayers have managed to generate a powerful response and have created something like breath that entered into the crevices of my being and changed things— either for me or someone else.

My favorite prayer of the moment is, "Lord . . . look down here," which comes from the novel *River Rising* by Athol Dickson. I like the simplicity of this prayer for so many reasons, but mostly it implies that the Lord will indeed look down, and that when he does, he will do so in grace and mercy. Yes, Lord, look down here indeed because we've got a heap of trouble.

I've prayed on my knees, lying in bed, hands folded at a

table, and driving down the highway. Usually, I pray quietly and alone. I'm not much for loud prayers or even for talking about prayer to others. But in spite of that, here I am now, praying for strangers, and opening up my heart, talking about prayer to you.

My best prayers have sometimes been the ones uttered at the end of my rope. Desolate and desperate prayers, usually with my head leaning on my steering wheel. Those prayers have been pretty much my "Lord, look down here" prayers. Or simply my relinquishing of the moment, realizing I really had no control over the situation. Then somehow sensing that God did indeed know how things were going to turn out in my current, desperate situation. And that, no matter what, he would be there.

What prayer has always meant to me was a direct line to God. But it has certainly never been a conversation starter with other people. Yet, prayer is proving to be just that—an introduction on my part that has the potential to possibly even build lasting relationships that go far beyond brief conversations and awkward introductions.

More than once a week I see Josh. He waves at me across the parking lot of the store I frequent, calling out, "Hi, River Jordan." I yell back, "Good to see you, man." Because it is. This is my friend Joshua. *My friend* is exactly what I call him and that's the way I would introduce him to you. I'm guessing we never would have spoken at any great length or depth except for the fact that once he helped me to the car with my bags and it just so happened I felt that he was to be my stranger for the day. It caused me to slow down in the situation like it always does. I had to stop rushing through the details of my to-do list, ask his name, and tell him what I was up to. I'll never forget his smile when I got to the part about praying for him. Then he asked my name and we had a genuine conversation. That was sometime back, and now, many conversations later, I am invested in his life. I know he has six children and four grandchildren and that he likes to fish. I know about his two jobs and his being laid off from one.

One evening he calls out my name but he seems down-trodden, not his usual cheerful self, and I ask him what's wrong. "Times are getting tough," he tells me. "My hours have been cut and we're having a really hard time making it." There's a lump in his throat when he shares this bit of news, and I must admit the most amazing thing—there's a lump in mine, too. I really care. Here is this person who normally would just barely be on my radar and now I not only know the details about his life, but I'm concerned that things go well for him. Our lives are connected in such a way that before, from just our passing hellos or thank-yous, would not have developed. What matters to Josh matters to me. What matters to me matters to him. He cares if my car breaks down. I care if his life is good or if he's going through hard times. "Don't worry," I tell him. "I'm going to say extra prayers for you and everything's going to work out all right."

"I sure hope so, River. And thank you. I sure appreciate it."

I've been thanked more already in this year of my life than all my years put together. For something so intangible and invisible as prayer.

Somewhere in my memory an odd fact surfaces that in one of the many old Native American languages one word for "friend," so I understand, translates to "One who carries my burden." If that's true, then indeed Josh is my friend because when I haven't seen him for a few days, I start asking around at the store. "Is he all right? Did he get a different job? I understand his hours have been cut."

Then I pull into the store tonight and hear a familiar "Hey, River Jordan!" And there he is with his usual grin. He reports that he's got a new morning job and he's able to keep this one, too. Things are looking up in his life. This is good news for the both of us.

What I know is that although I've picked up others' burdens along the way, they have continually lightened mine. I've met so many wonderful people and I won't ever forget them. I see them now at the oddest times, a face I'd thought I'd forgotten. A person who stopped and turned around just like Josh did that first night and asked, "Wait a minute, what is your name?" There it is, that snapshot of him as he pushes shopping carts across a dark parking lot, a summer night hanging over him. When I am an old, old woman, I will remember his face and the face of all these strangers at odd times. These people and their stories will come back to me as good company. I never imagined that this world of relationships, of friendships, was only a prayer away.

THE MISFITS

There are thoughts which are prayers.
There are moments when, whatever the
posture of the body, the soul is on its knees.

—VICTOR HUGO

I've GOT ENOUGH TROUBLE. LOOMING MEDICAL TESTS AND worries of my own. Odd pains that reveal something that isn't normal, but right now "not normal" is a cloudy concept. So I'm waiting out the results of kidney scans to see if the news is good or something more to worry about. But I have a resolution to cast my eyes off my own worries to search the crowd for a stranger, and in doing so, my spirit softens to the day. If I'm to pray for a stranger today from the public, then it will be someone here, in this store I'm shopping in before I go home to write again.

A man calls to me from the sidewalk, "Hello." It's a different kind of hello. It's the kind that would make some people walk faster to get away. When I look up at him and say, "Hi," I see why.

He's built a little different than most people. One eye is slightly lower than the other, and the rest of his face a little off-kilter as well, as if it was never quite finished, clay that was cast aside in the creative process. His body is extra large but hangs at odd angles. His pants are up above his ankles, his white socks showing prominently. I ask him how he's doing and he says, "Fine." Then I walk inside the store and think he's my stranger but I don't slow down. First, I figure me talking to him, telling him that I was praying for him today, might offend him in some way. But then I decide it's the right thing to do anyway. By the time I meet my sister, exchange things, leave the store, he's no longer there. But I don't forget him. I come home and pray for him and his great big hellos. For daring to speak to people, to strangers on the street. I pray that he have a friend, a really good friend in his life. Someone he can count on and who sees the light of who he really is.

Then I pray for the lonely and for those that this world considers ugly because they don't fit the happy, beautiful mold that we've created. For the lost, cast aside, and rejected in this world. I pray that God bring them friends. Really wonderful friends. And that he helps me become one. My husband says that I'm a misfit magnet anyway.

"They find you like a moth to a flame. Somehow you must just call to them."

I can't exactly argue. But then J. D. Salinger has been called the Patron Saint of Misfits and Outcasts. That's a grand title and the kind of office I wouldn't mind holding. All of this helps me stop thinking about myself. At least for a moment or two out of my day. But I could tell my husband the other reason the misfits find me, circle, feel comfortable, and land nearby. I'm one of them. They sense that. I'm the kid on the outside looking in, or the inside looking out depending on where everyone else is playing. I'm the woman years ago who managed to walk through an entire mall with her skirt tucked into the back of her panty hose after leaving the restroom. Oh, the misfit stories, they're a dime a dozen with my name stamped on them. But the misfits don't need the stories. They have a sixth sense. They recognize me.

Much to my delight when I return to the store the following week, he's actually working there, is proudly wearing the company shirt and name tag. I still don't stop him but I come home and tell my husband, *Do you know who got a job?! The misfit man.*

The fact is in the middle of my worries and concerns, yet again, one more time, one more day—God has been able to pull me out of my own skin and obsession with my life to care deeply for a person that I don't know and may never see again. How deeply and for how long? Does it matter? I believe a passionate three minutes are much more powerful than a life of lukewarm ambivalence.

In the ensuing weeks, the man keeps his job, and he and my husband become used to their own personal banter—an odd type of communication they create where they understand one another. We attend a community picnic one day and find our friend walking the crowd at his strange, awkward pace. I step up, surprised and delighted to see him—what? Out? On his own more or less. "Hey," I tell him, "how you doing?" He recognizes what I believe is the genuine tone of my voice. He grabs my hand, shakes it profusely, and offers me a "Happy New Year!" with great enthusiasm even though it's a hot, humid day and January is months away. It's his form of prayer as far as I care. A blessing from the man. He's wishing me goodness with his whole heart. I'll take that every day of the year. "Happy New Year!" I reply and I mean it with all my might.

FERVOR AND FIRE

**Prayer, like radium, is a luminous and
self-generating form of energy.**

—DR. ALEXIS CARREL

A BRIGHT, SHINING STAR, THAT'S WHAT SHE IS. IT'S WHAT strikes me, makes me smile when I start to walk past her. She's striking up a chord for heavenly needs on this side of earth. Of all things a favorite quote from Jack Kerouac comes to mind—

The only people for me are the mad ones, the ones who are mad to live, mad to talk, mad to be saved, desirous of everything at the same time, the ones who never yawn or say a commonplace thing, but burn, burn, burn like fabulous yellow roman candles exploding like spiders across the stars and in the middle you see the blue center light pop and everybody goes "Awww!"

It's that kind of pent-up, just contained zeal. She's working outside the front of the store collecting contributions for a children's ministry. And she's clapping her hands, singing a song, pacing back and forth a little, a rhythm to her dance. I smile as I walk past her, then I turn around and walk back to her. It seems like this is how it's going to be this year, always turning around midstep, midstream. I introduce myself and ask her name.

"Estelle," she says with a wink and a quick wave as if she is still keeping time to a beat only she can hear.

I explain my prayer year to her, of the people I meet and about how they stand out to me, special people every day. I tell her today she is my person. The twinkle in her eye explodes like Kerouac lights. They burn brighter, hotter, and take me in with a fresh assessment.

"And what's your name?" she asks me.

Then she tells me she is going to be praying for me, too. "Matter of fact," she says, "I'm gonna pray for you right now!"

They burn, burn, burn, these people like Estelle. You can see their light a mile away. Somehow they remain fearless. And if they are bruised by life, they don't show it.

Grabs me, she does. This spitfire little woman about the size of my Aunt Leaner, who could move mountains with her whiplike words. Estelle grabs my hand and pulls me closer to her. Then she prays for me, reminding me so much of Esther, the homeless woman from the park.

But the first thing that hits me is, *Don't pray for me in public, pray for me later, like I do!* I'm aware that there are people walking in and out of the door behind me, people crossing the parking lot, people everywhere. Self-conscious? Like a third grader forced into a talent show in front of the entire school.

Then something surprising happens in spite of old memories and self-conscious moments: When the words roll off her tongue, when I hear the balm of those words rushing over me, her asking for goodness in my life, for my direction to be clear, my destiny to be perfectly fulfilled, I want to say, *Pray on! Go ahead. Say another prayer for me, Estelle.* But suddenly she's wrapped up her prayer for me as quickly as she started.

She smiles and steps back from me. "I'll pray for you again when God brings you to mind," she tells me. "I won't even need to remember your name; I'll see your face and I'll know."

And just like that she echoes what has been happening to me so far this year. Faces coming to mind, faces of so many people I've connected with for a moment or prayed for silently without ever speaking to them. So it could be like that, I think. Each of us praying for strangers, remembering them, praying for them again. Forever. Perhaps it's part of some great possibility. Today as I watch the news from around the world, I hope it is. And I am thankful that there are people in this world full of fire, fearless in their faith, willing to remember and oblige with a blessing.

IN FEAR AND TREMBLING

Courage is fear that has said its prayers.

—DOROTHY BERNARD

WHY AM I SO AFRAID? ALL I WANT TO DO IS SPEAK TO A stranger, to tell them that I'm praying for them. That they stood out to me in a special way, that there's a part of me that will never forget them. I've been doing this for months now and still—I tremble.

I'm watching a woman in a restaurant where I'm having dinner. She's getting many phone calls, stepping outside, pacing and talking on her phone. It's margarita night and her table has a few pitchers. I see her through the window. I try to just eat, not to watch her, not to be aware. Then I get over my inability to ignore the fact that she is my stranger and try to just figure out one more time how I'll manage approaching and talking to a stranger out of the blue.

I'm not the kind of woman to fear many things. Not that I don't have a disposition that genetically leads to worry about my family because that I do. I fight that all the time. But fearful—not really. I travel alone; don't fear storms or things that go bump in the night. But telling a stranger that they'll be in my heart and in my thoughts before I go to sleep, well, what a scary thing. And I think the reason for it is a deep-seated human emotion that desires not to be rejected. For someone to think that I'm crazy, off-center, out of bounds. But then—even writing those words, I really don't care if anyone thinks I'm crazy. I write Southern Gothic fiction and most of the characters in the novels have a touch of the unusual, the eccentric. I consider them good company, and for a Southern novelist, being a tad different can be just part of the badge of being a great writer.

But out-and-out rejection by people when it's not related to writing in any form, well, that's another story. Maybe it's that talent show I endured in the third grade when I played the piano for a crowd of giggling classmates. I lost the talent contest to a girl doing a tap dance in a tutu. Lost by a landslide. The votes were counted aloud and marked in white chalk one by one next to our names on the board. I received two votes. One of them was mine. Shortly thereafter I begged my mother to let me quit. She finally gave in, for which I now give her the hardest of times. I discovered years later that the piano teacher thought I had real talent, showed promise, that I was the best student she had ever taught. Now, all I can do with those lessons is type fast, but at least that comes in pretty handy.

I'm thinking somewhere in my soul, as I approach strangers, an echo of that third grade rejection keeps repeating itself. It's the same rejection any of us experiences when teams were picked in PE and we weren't called out very early. The same one when we miss the first spelling word and have to sit down right away in the firing squad ritual referred to as a spelling bee. Sometimes I think what I was supposed to learn from these childhood experiences was that I could indeed survive. I'm not sure that was my take away. What I think I learned was if you want to be popular, get a tutu.

"Excuse me, but do you mind if I ask your name?" I jump in before I can remember to be afraid.

Margarita Lady has been drinking, the kind of drinking where maybe someone gets mean. I've been in enough bars to recognize how people can turn one way or the other after a few too many. I've been watching her, trying to figure out how to approach her, and she's been watching me back. She probably thinks I've been judging her, sizing her up, giving her black marks. I haven't been. I have nothing against tequila, as long as someone takes the car keys away from her.

On my way out of the restaurant, I kneel down beside her where she's with a large group of people possibly celebrating something. When I ask her name, she gives me a stony look, turns to her friend, and says, "She wants to know my name." There is a strong sarcastic tone attached to that statement. It doesn't matter to me. This is my response:

"Look, you don't really have to tell me your name. I stopped by because I have a resolution. I pray for a stranger every day and today you're my stranger."

"Well, isn't that nice?" Same dripping sarcastic tone.

"I'll be wishing you special blessings tonight before I go to sleep. For all the good things you're hoping for in life to be fulfilled. That's all. Take care."

The major trick in the whole few minutes this occurred was that I really meant what I said. I still meant it when I went to bed thinking of her and wishing for a deep healing in the dark places, for her health and happiness. I meant it with a peculiar passion. Because it really isn't about someone getting mushy and giving me hugs, it's about the fact that praying for strangers is helping me become a better human being. I do this for me.

THE BACKSTABBERS

God be kind to all good Samaritans and also bad ones.
For such is the kingdom of Heaven.

—JOHN GARDNER

PART OF THIS PRAYING FOR STRANGERS RESOLUTION IS THAT I never know what to expect. Let's face it, accosting strangers does add a serious element of adventure to your average day.

This time I'm walking out of the cell phone store when someone grabs my attention. As it so often seems to happen, I pass someone as I'm walking through the doors, having completed one more thing on my list. And I suppose, in some ways, the motion of the passing has made it easier for me to stop the person. Today that's what I do as I begin to pass a woman but slow my step and say, "Excuse me." Then I tell her my story.

She tells me her name is Beth and says, "It's interesting that you stopped me today of all days. I just left my office and there are people there I am working with, you know? People who are—ohhh, you have to be so careful, I tell you. You can't turn your back on nobody. Why does it have to be like that? I am so upset." She stomps her foot. She's a petite woman, a real firecracker. I wouldn't want her mad at me, and now she seems to be full of righteous indignation.

"I understand," I say. That's an understatement. I've had my soul bruised black by betrayal.

"Funny you stopped me. How did you know?"

"I don't know." I pat her on the shoulder, "But hey, it'll work out. Everything will be all right." What I mean by that is, *Honey, we survive the scars where when our backs were turned, we caught more than our share from friends we trusted. Life goes on.* We learn, and sometimes in the learning unfortunately we compensate, draw back a little, slow ourselves to trust a neighbor. I'm thinking I understand better than she knows. More than she ever needs to know. It's a fresh wound for me as well, although it happened a while back. Just last night that betrayal was brought back to me and it still stung.

It was after dinner when I realized that I hadn't prayed for anyone during the day. And it left me as empty and aged as old sin. Swear. I hadn't felt that kind of void since I don't know when. It's the kind of empty that can eat at my soul. First I was busy. Just busy. Busy with my life. Enjoying my morning with my husband, hustling to get my radio program produced, rushing to the studio, and then enjoying being with listeners. Then I came home, sat down, and it hit me—it was pushing 7 p.m. and I hadn't met anyone, or prayed for anyone today. So then I tried to snatch names out of the air. I was wandering around pretty antsy, searching for someone to pray for. Wandering through the house wondering if I had missed someone along the way.

My husband came across an old, canceled check cashed by a man who stole money from us. And that is the flat-out truth. At the time it was our life savings. Everything. My husband's attitude was better than mine. One of forgiveness and prayer. That special grace didn't fall on me. I wanted—not revenge, mind you, because after all, money is only paper in the end—but some kind of justice enacted. Or at least I wanted the man to feel sorry for what he'd done. He was a con man, all right, although his work and he personally had been recommended by a friend of a friend. The bitter taste left in my mouth from the entire incident lingered even as my husband and I had prospered. Bitter like bile rising up. Okay, maybe there was just a touch of righteous anger there. The audacity of a swindler and all that. So my husband turned to me and said, "Hey, here's a name from the past. Remember this man? Have you prayed for him lately?"

"Who?" I asked him, and then it hit me. I remembered the man and the situation. "Oh, that guy! No, prayer isn't what comes to mind." And I might have added a few more thoughts about the situation, with my husband saying something like, "Oh, it's all right."

I continued through the night trying to think of someone who might need a prayer other than my immediate family. I was feeling empty. I'd grown accustomed to having something that attached me to the human race outside the small window of my personal existence.

I tried to reassure myself that my unbroken leading, my resolution, this thing I was doing had not been nullified or jinxed like a stupid old chain letter. I tried to calm myself with the idea that maybe it was just a good night to pray in general. Maybe a blanket prayer for the end of wars, or for the homeless to find refuge, for the innocent to be protected. But the itch didn't settle.

My unforgivingness had led me straight down to a dark corridor. And the unforgivingness in my heart was so locked up, so much like stone, that my husband's turning to me and saying, "Have you prayed for him lately?" didn't even faze me. I guess that's how unforgivingness can be. Cornering us into a dark part of our soul.

Soon it was ten o'clock at night and I was still searching. Maybe I was the one who needed prayer. Maybe I should have been about the business of the condition of my heart. My guess was that this man would work it all out with God in due time. And I truly and prayerfully wished him, as well as myself, great mercy.

It was a lesson learned. One that I hope I can pass on. To let Beth know for certain that betrayal and the poison of backstabbers, gossipers, and mean-spirited people do not have to rule the day or change our hearts.

I smile at Beth and say, "Maybe we're just supposed to forgive them and move on. Who knows?"

"What a good idea, you know? This prayer thing." She nods her head as if her mind is made up. "I like it." She touches my arm tentatively, a new look in her eye. "You know, I'm going to do this. Me, too. I'll do it, too."

I'm walking to the car when she calls after me, "You know, maybe I'll even pray for those women at work. Like you say—who knows? Maybe it will change things."

I look back at Beth and smile. I wave good-bye and drive away smiling because it's one of those times when interrupting someone's life feels like it was really worth the time. I've got a laundry list of names I could pray for in the wake of her comment. A long list of untrustable folks I put my trust in. That was my mistake. Age helps that. You get to where you can see a thing coming a mile away. You can smell a storm on the horizon, recognize a type, and learn to follow your instincts. This prayer thing, I could tell her, I like it, too. It helps keep me glued back to a humanity that I could have turned my face away from so many times. It helps me meet this foot-stomping woman walking through the wake of that refuge of an ugly morning. But something tells me the rest of her day went a little better than planned, and mine did, too.

TRAVELS AND TRAVAILS—
PART ONE

**Walking with God down the avenue of
prayer we acquire something of His likeness;
and unconsciously we become witnesses to
others of His beauty and His grace.**

—E. M. BOUNDS

I'VE HAD A LITTLE CAR TROUBLE ON THE ROAD. NO, I'VE HAD more than a little. More than my fair share. The trusty little Nissan Altima that has carried me more than two hundred fifty thousand faithful miles has given up the ghost. No fault of my own like in times past when my old Volvo's oil had turned to sludge mud until the engine froze. No, sir. The Nissan was tuned up, oil changed, new tires, and I was thousands of miles from home when she died.

For the record, I'm a car girl. Have been since I was first bestowed that little white convertible, push-pedal car that happened to match my mother's white convertible. But the cars I drive don't always represent the cars I love. They can't. I love old pickup trucks and American muscle cars, VW bugs, and '57 Chevies, hot-off-the-line Chevy 300s, Porches, and snappy new Kias. I love them all. I have happy memories on the road as a child, and maybe that's why I don't mind rambling from one city's bookstore to another, reading and signing for a recent release. And I don't require a brand-new car every year to carry me there. I get a little attached to vehicles like a cowgirl might a pony, and so I rode that baby right into the sunset.

Then I was stuck in the middle of what you might call nowhere. I had stopped at a grocery store in a small town on the back side of the North Carolina coast on my way to another book signing. When I got back in my car and turned the ignition key, I knew something didn't sound right at all. Farther down the road the noise became the kind of sound that made me say something brilliant like, "Uh-oh."

I drove to the closest store I could pull into, parked the car, and walked inside uttering to the crowd of innocent bystanders, "Can someone please tell me where I am?" While it might be a great question for theological or psychological discussion, what I meant very simply was what town have I found myself in? Exactly, geographically, where am I? I made a note to self to break down and buy one of those GPS thingies. I think the people in the store visibly relaxed when I followed up by pointing my finger over my shoulder and asking, "And does anyone know anything at all about cars?"

Two men, one my daddy's age, one my son's age, follow me out the door and say, "Okay, start her up." I did. It took just a minute for both of them to shake their heads and remark that this didn't sound good. And that's exactly what they said. The younger man said, "That doesn't sound good." And the older man says, "No, it doesn't. It sure doesn't."

The younger man has to leave but the older one sticks around and we begin talking.

"I'm retired," he says. He doesn't have to say retired from what because the way he stands, back straight, more or less at attention, and those tattoos on his arm are a dead giveaway. My daddy was military. I know that look, that air a man carries when he has spent a lifetime both giving and following orders.

"What branch?"

"Army. Spent twenty-two years."

"My daddy, too," I say. "Got both sons deployed now."

"Iraq?"

"One there and one in Afghanistan."

He looks down, shaking his head. "Got a mess on our hands is what we got."

He's not talking about the car anymore. Just the whole picture of war. He reminds me so much of my father, who passed away a few years ago. He's got all that retired Army feeling to him, even some of the same mannerisms. I could swear there's the scent of Old Spice lingering in the air.

"Listen," he tells me. "You are in a place where after five o'clock you can't get anywhere from here. Now there's an auto parts place down the street that does a good job. Those guys can tell you what's up and maybe somewhere you can get it fixed that you can trust."

He starts giving me directions, but by the time he gets to the third red light, my mind is somewhere else. I'm already hearing Simon and Garfunkel singing "Homeward Bound" and trying to figure out how I'm gonna get out of this mess. The soldier must have noticed the glazed look in my eye.

"Never mind." He walks to his truck and motions. "Follow me. I'm going to lead you there. Now when I give you the signal, you turn off. That'll be the place."

"Got it. Thank you, sir." And I'm whispering under my breath, "And today you are my stranger." I figure there's no point in confusing the issue. The man is on a mission to help me get fixed and back on the road.

A few miles down the road and one bridge later I see the sign of an auto place in front of me. I blow my horn thanks, creep into the parking lot with the engine clanking and rattling. I'm still there, standing in line, waiting to be helped, when I look up and see old sarge come through the doors, shaking his head. He walks up to me and whispers, "Whatchu doin here? I didn't give you the signal. This ain't the place."

"Sorry, sorry," I tell him and follow him out the door.

"On down the road," he tells me and I get in the car and pull out behind him.

A few miles down the road he gives me a clear-cut signal, honking his horn and pointing for me to turn into the parking lot of another auto parts store. I watch the taillights of his truck pull away as I wave bye out the window. I want to say, *Oh, never mind this car business. I'm tired and need some time to think. Let's park this thing and I'll just go on home with you and meet the missus. Maybe have a spot of supper and stay the night at your house. If nothing else, let me catch up to you and tell you about this thing I do, about how you are my stranger.*

It doesn't work out that way, of course. I sit there with my blinker on and watch that truck make the next curve and disappear from sight. Then I take a little time to pray for that man. Oh, yes I do. And I am exceedingly grateful.

TRAVELS AND TRAVAILS— PART TWO

Prayer moves the hand that moves the universe.

—ANONYMOUS

SOMETIMES IT'S NOT UNTIL ALL HELL BREAKS LOOSE, UNTIL you break down, get lost, lose your place in life in general, that you discover angels abounding everywhere. I've now had seven more people listen to my car and say, "That doesn't sound good." Then as if to validate their opinion, the engine makes one last grinding noise and stops altogether. I'm thinking this little pony has taken her last ride. Yes, chances are her last giddyap is gone, gone, but there'll be time for memories later. Right now, I'm stranded. With complications.

I'm supposed to be on the way to the cabin of a friend who has graciously offered me an opportunity to stay there and write, free of charge. God bless her and all the people far and wide who open their doors to writers and artists of all kinds who must disappear to create. So this is where I'm going, this is the plan, but it has left me in a jam. I can't do anything with my car, and renting a car to just sit for a month in the woods doesn't make sense. Ultimately, I will have to replace my car—that is, if the car is really history, kaput, over, finished.

So now I just find a tow truck and arrange for the car to be towed from nowhere to somewhere back over the bridge to a shop that supposedly knows how to work on Nissan engines. Then I call a cab, unload all my writerly stuff and suitcases, and reload them into the cab.

"And if you don't mind, buddy, I'll just ride up front with you."

Riding in the backseat right now feels too passive. There's nothing like being stuck on the back roads of America to make you feel out of control. Hiking the trail west might be an alternative if I were not traveling with a laptop, fourteen books, and enough clothes for a month. Traveling the back roads of America without a car is really not an option.

Strangers, I'm thinking. *Think of the strangers*. But I'm the stranger here. I'm the one needing some divine intervention. It reminds me of another retreat, one where I'd been alone for weeks, writing, missing my husband, and when I went out for supplies, I realized how very tired and hungry I was. It was then I realized that as much as I can be alone for long periods of time, as much as I can enjoy solitude and the creative space it allows me to work, it might just be nice to have a stranger invite me in for a bowl of soup, a crust of bread, and a little conversation. I can't convey to you how much I wanted this on that particular lonely, tired, and hungry evening. But that moment serves to remind me that other people experience this so often. Longing for just a touch, a shared meal, and a few words.

I take a deep breath and try not to focus on the car I left behind or what I can figure out tomorrow. Instead, I focus on the cabdriver and begin to ask him questions about his own life as we drive miles and miles to another city. And as the meter burns up my road trip dollars, he begins to tell me things. I settle back and listen. There's not much else to do.

He's had a hundred lives; this one is just another chapter but probably his last. He's a smoker and I can tell he's trying not to smoke right now. I guess he reserves that for when he is waiting for a call. I figure I'm one of the longest fares he's had in a while. He had to come over the bridge from another city to get me and now we're headed back the same way.

"You got reservations?"

"I got nothing," I tell him. "Except what I just loaded in your cab."

We're crossing the bridge now and I look out over the water thinking of people on journeys everywhere, getting stranded from one bad thing or another that happens. We drive awhile in silence. It's seven o'clock at night, places have closed, mechanics have gone to bed, and tow trucks won't go over the bridge to get my car, or what's left of it, until tomorrow.

"And that's how I ended up here," I hear him saying.

"Is that so?" I have no idea what he just told me. I missed that part of his story worrying about mine.

"There's a hotel up here that doesn't cost so much. It's old but it's all right."

"Sounds fine. Anything will do right now."

He pulls up to what I might have figured was one of those old Florida roadside hotels. The kind that used to have the Magic Fingers beds, where you could put a quarter in the box above the bed and it would shake like crazy for about five minutes. Then I'd beg my mother for another quarter. I could use some magic fingers right now. And a whirlpool, a hot toddy, and a train ticket out of here.

The desk clerk is delighted to have another customer. The cab waits on me to check in and get a key, then he pulls around to Room 12. A few guys are sitting outside of the room with a cooler in between them drinking beer. Lovely. I pay the cabdriver, pull my cases into the room, and lock the door. Okay, I've been in better. The Queen Elizabeth in Montreal comes to mind. But then I've also slept on the top of a van in the middle of an alligator swamp.

I'm tempted to just stay here locked in my room, but my stomach grumbles and I'm reminded I haven't eaten anything since breakfast. This certainly isn't a place that has room service so I make my way back to the front office to find out my options. Those good ole boys drinking their beer don't even give me a second look. The desk clerk informs me that the Thai restaurant next door is incredible. As he passes me a paper menu, he remarks, "You don't look like you're on vacation exactly."

"Honey, right now I'm sure I don't look like a lot of things." I am so worn out and heavy hearted. I'm under deadline, deadline, deadline for my new novel and that fact is beating on my brain. And my month in this cabin that I can't get to now has just been postponed by a day or two. Finally, I blurt the words from my brain. "I'm under deadline," I tell the desk clerk, "for my next novel."

"You're a writer? A novelist?"

"On my better days. Here's a bookmark with a picture taken where I looked a little less . . ."

"Broken down?"

"Yes, that would do it, a little less broken down."

"Nice picture."

"Really, it's all smoke and mirrors, you know? Lighting or something."

"A real writer staying here with us, imagine that."

"Do you like to read?" I'm making small talk, looking at the paper menu. Mentally choosing between pad Thai or tofu and vegetables.

"I read everything. I *love* to read."

"Like what?" Tofu, definitely tofu and vegetables.

"Chekhov."

I put the menu down and look at this desk clerk, this man, in the middle of nowhere, at this crumbling roadside motel.

"I love Chekhov and I've recently been reading . . ."

Then we talk. Really talk. We discuss his current reading list, his favorites, and the reasons why he loves them. The man has an incredible passion for literature and a beautiful way of describing a writer's prose, the long-lasting meaning of the story. He's more than well read. He's exceptional.

"You should be teaching," I tell him. But who am I to tell someone what he should be doing with his life? Who would have thought a desk clerk at this hotel was reading plays, great literature, Pulitzer Prize winners and runners-up? Not me. But I'm learning every broken-down step of the way not to assume I know someone's complete story. Not to assume that their lot in life, their position, their job, will tell me about their secret passions.

"I'm so glad I met you," I tell him. For so many reasons I mean that most sincerely. And I've prayed for my stranger for the day but that doesn't matter. After I've eaten spicy Thai, after I've pushed the bureau over in front of the door, after I've turned out the only working light—I say a special prayer for that cabdriver. Another one for Harry, the desk clerk. I pray that his life will be filled with words, the stories he loves, and that there will be an open door in his life where he can share that passion.

"Matter of fact," I say aloud, "as long as I'm at it, I'm going to pray for everyone that crossed my path today. *Everyone.*" And then I turn out the light, and fall asleep listening for noises outside my door, and not so much worried about my deadline anymore.

TRAVELS AND TRAVAILS—
PART THREE

**God answers sharp and sudden on some prayers,
and thrusts the thing we have prayed for in
our face, a gauntlet with a gift in't.**

—ELIZABETH BARRETT BROWNING

THE SIDE TRIP ADVENTURE CONTINUES. MY DAUGHTER-IN-law has loaded up the adorables, respectively seven and two, and is coming to rescue me from my picturesque road stop and take me to their house.

The beer cooler man, apparently my room neighbor, meets me outside this morning asking, "How's it going?"

I answer him while still walking toward the hotel office. "Car broke down but it'll get better."

He leans back against a pole and eyes me. "Well, that explains it."

"What's that?"

"Well, I ain't never seen a woman pull up at a motel in a taxicab before."

"Is that a fact?"

"Yep, you are for sure the first."

"Well." I smile, thinking he hasn't been in Manhattan lately. Or Chicago. Or Dallas, Miami, LA, Grand Rapids, and because I just don't think it's time to go into all that, I say, "You take care."

"Have a goodun," I hear as I'm walking away.

A few days later I have verified that a one-way flight on short notice is basically a million dollars and some odd cents. The train that used to run between here and there no longer stops at the closest city. Rental car companies are being moody—they don't want to rent one-way today. I'm searching for a clunker to buy to get me to that cabin and through the next thirty days. My writing clock is ticking, time's wasting. It has been determined that, yes, indeed, my car is parts now. Good for nothing more than vulture pickings from the junkyard. She's a goner but she's been, as the man says, a goodun.

If I were simply going home to Nashville, this would be one plane ticket and I'd be done, but I'm determined to follow through with my plans to hide and write. My son calls from Afghanistan with the idea that I should take his truck as it is just sitting there. "Needs to be driven anyway."

Great idea. This could work. "I'd take it in, just to get checked out, before you go. Just to be sure," my son suggests. And so I do. I take it to a mechanic a few towns over that he recommends and ask, "Excuse me, but could you just listen to this little noise before I drive states away?"

"Ma'am, you won't even make it out of the city with this truck. It needs a thingamoohooch." Or at least that's what I thought he said. And as he is readying up some sort of estimate, as I am calling my husband, as I'm sitting with my head in my hands at an outside picnic table, I'm thinking, *Strangers. Don't forget the strangers.* But I'm the stranger needing prayer, my inner voice is arguing back. *Me, me, me.*

"Sure hope this isn't what I think it is," a man pacing outside next to me says. I look up; shelter my eyes from the sun. He looks worried. "You got a car in there, too?" he asks.

"See that car?" I point to where the truck is sweetly parked. "It's history. Couldn't make an inch much less a mile."

"Sure sorry about that. Whatchugonnado?" He says it just like that. Turns the phrase into one word.

"Well, I'm not sure. Waiting now to find out about another ride."

"Lord, I hope I don't need another ride, you know? Money's been tight as it is."

"Listen, I do this thing. Where I pray for a stranger every day, so I'll be thinking about you, hoping that it all works out for your car and everything. You know?"

"Well, I sure do appreciate that. I sure do need that."

"What's your name?"

"Thomas." I repeat it, write it down. I now have names spilling out of me everywhere.

His car comes around the corner. And he gets in to go with the mechanic on a test drive. "Thanks again, Ms. Jordan. I do so appreciate those prayers."

"Me, too," I whisper to the air. Because I am exhausted, drained, and yes, need a few well-felt prayers.

The owner of the shop has been working on the truck and is now out taking it for a test drive. I check my watch, wonder how long it might take me to cross state lines, how late that I can drive into the night. *Pray for all the strangers*, I keep thinking. And I'm thinking it still when I see the shop owner come walking down the street and back to where I'm standing.

"You won't believe this," he starts.

"Oh, I think I will. It's been that kind of week."

"Well, it would be better for you to just come look. That will explain it." He walks me down the street and points around the corner.

"Is that my truck there?"

"That's it. Have never had one do that to me. Wheels just about came off completely."

The truck looks like it's kneeling, the hood fallen down to follow the line of the wheels, which are both bent sideways at broken angles like odd bones in wrong places. I just shake my head and go back to the picnic table. The man follows me.

"We've had to call a tow truck to come pull it out of the road."

"Uh-huh."

"But that won't get you anywhere tonight."

My budget for this writing retreat excursion is being sucked into a black hole. I call my husband, and simply pass the phone to the shop man. I can't speak right now. I'm in what might not be considered the best side of town, the middle of nowhere, encircled by seedy bars. The closest family is three cities away and my productive, lush idea of hiding and writing is fading fast.

"No, she's taking it real good. She's being really nice," I hear the man saying. What I'm trying not to do is cry. He passes me the phone and my husband tries to comfort me as best he can from a thousand miles away. Then the man offers me one of his personal cars to get somewhere. Probably anywhere, so that I'm not sitting at that picnic table locked up in the fence all night long.

"I appreciate it," I tell him and I really do.

Three hours later I'm back at my daughter-in-law's door driving the loaner. She has lit candles in my honor. Poured red wine. She has tried her best to soothe this incredulous road trip mayhem. And I feel so stupidly blessed. In the middle of all these mishaps, I have been surrounded by a worn-out peace that I swear I would ascribe to this simple resolution. In the middle of everything, it has been keeping me balanced and sane as I look beyond my own circumstances.

The truck is fixed a few days later to the tune of almost a thousand dollars and I'm on the road again, eventually arriving at my destination, where I rarely drive except when the lack of basic supplies forces me to put down the laptop and drive out of the woods, down the dirt roads, a lonely highway to another lonely highway to the nearest place for food.

In the end, I've left a string of people pearled across my path. There was a reader who offered to carry me halfway across a state to her brother's house, a waitress who befriended me, a truck driver and his wife who would have carried me to Albuquerque, the cabdriver with old stories, a man who ran a general store who showed such concern, and a hotel clerk named Harry who had such a wild passion for literature we could have talked all night.

"To all your travels and travails," Dr. Yolanda Reed, my writing mentor, once toasted us playwrights at the end of a writing workshop. *What a strange toast*, I thought at the time. That was twenty years ago. Now, I understand. *Yes, to all our travels and travails, indeed. And to the special strangers we meet along the way.*

CABINS CONFESSIONS

**When I pray, coincidences happen,
and when I don't pray, they don't.**

—WILLIAM TEMPLE

So I am on my writer's retreat. I use the word *RETREAT* loosely. I feel more like I am on lock-down, missing my family, my dog, and television. I'm in my friend's cabin in the north woods of South Carolina for my self-imposed isolation. This is supposed to be ideal for a writer under deadline. No phones to answer, no contact, no bills to pay, no dishes to wash. I don't even have to speak to anyone. It should be a serene, creative haven where safety isn't a concern and where I can tap into my imagination without reservation about things that go bump in the night—or bite. It doesn't feel that way. To the owner's flabbergasted dismay, the cabin has become infested with scorpions. The kind that sting—hard. Not poisonous enough to kill, but enough to be painful or make you ill. I've found them waiting for me in the morning by my pillow; I've been killing at least four a day and now have pulled the mattresses away from the walls so that they might be discouraged from crawling the bed legs to join me. I feel as though I am sleeping on a life raft, waking throughout the night to check the sheets and my body for fluorescent creatures of desert dominion. It was a battle getting to this place, and now the battle continues. It's left my soul tired. And maybe a little mean.

I decide to escape for a few hours, to leave *The Miracle of Mercy Land*—the novel I'm writing—for a while and seek green trees and fresh air. I crank the loaned truck and take off toward the state park twelve country road miles away. I park the truck and trudge through the humidity to the ranger's hut, thinking I'll collect more information on the park in general, and camping, more specifically, in detail. I'm thinking I need a rocky vista overlook where my husband might come visit me on this self-imposed exile to write. Maybe he could bring the big white dog, and we'd pitch a tent. That all sounds so warm and wonderful because really, at this point, I'm in need of something like a shoulder to cry on. Even if that crying is done in a sleeping bag hanging on the edge of a mountain.

The park ranger is gruff, to say the least. It's as if he doesn't want to talk to me. He doesn't want to tell me any stories about the place. He grunts and points to the rack of brochures. I was kind of fine up until then, but somewhere in the middle of his attitude, my attitude shifted. I take off walking the nature trail with a scowl on my face, a tired and angry cloud on my trail. Perhaps, even though scorpions haven't stung me yet, they are still winning the battle.

I'm hiking along in one of those places that is uphill in every direction, thinking about what a horrible, horrible man the park ranger is, judging him solidly in the process. Two young hikers pass me wearing big, cheery smiles and say hello. And *I don't even respond.* Not a smile, not a grunt, not even a simple, Southern nod of the hair. I'm too busy thinking alternately about the work on my book and on the grumpy-hearted man in the ranger's hut.

I finally come out of the woods from the hike, spider webs on my arms, hot, sweaty (of which I am never), and I rush into the women's room to wash my face and the back of my neck.

A woman comes in wearing hiker's gear. The real kind—real shorts that breathe and real boots that grip. Her hair is pulled back in a baseball cap. She's washing her hands and I can feel her trying to make contact with me. Do you know that feeling where someone is looking at you? Isn't it amazing how we can feel eyes upon us? I try to dry my face with paper towels, looking into the mirror, working hard to keep my eyes locked in place and not make eye contact with her.

We both exit the bathroom at the same time, and by the time I make it back to where the truck is parked, start it up, and pull through the driveway, she is there standing beside her husband by their car. My unfriendliness washes over me. All of it. The girls on the hike, the woman in the restroom, and my judging of the park ranger. Maybe the man's mother just died. Maybe his wife left him. How do we know these things about another person or the reasons for their behavior? The only behavior I have at least some control over at this point in life is my own.

I make a point of rolling down the window, smiling, and raising my hand in a wave. The woman immediately smiles back with such genuine sincerity and what I see is forgiveness.

I just love strangers! This thought wells up from a deep spring in my heart. It is pure in this moment of revelation and clarity. Then I begin to laugh as I pull away because the fact of the matter is my behavior over the last two hours has proved otherwise. There has been nothing stranger-loving about me. Until that last, redeeming moment.

I don't love all strangers all the time, that's for certain. But maybe, little by little, I'm learning to love strangers, love *people*, more every day.

COMMON GROUND

I do not intend to quit. I want to get along with you.
That is my prayer, to find common ground.

—MARGARET CRAFT

IT SEEMS THAT ALL THE THINGS I'VE LEARNED, SURVIVED, AND joylessly experienced in life now come back to me in a story. There is a great episode from *Star Trek: The Next Generation* where the captain is kidnapped and sent to a foreign planet to fight a common enemy alongside the captain of another race. At the end, the alien captain is dying, but Captain Picard comes to realize that because their people in the generations following will always have the story of them fighting together for a common cause, there will always be peace between them. The key element that is most crucial is their story. It's what their people will have to carry forward for years to come. Now that little TV episode from so many years ago comes back in echo form. The way that I compare what I'm experiencing now is remembering another story from my past or one that someone has told me. Even words of truth plucked from fictional stories. As the great Jack Reed has said, "You have to have heroes in life. It doesn't matter if they come from real life or the pages of fiction— you just have to have heroes." His personal hero of all time was Atticus Finch. Either him or Gregory Peck. Mr. Reed wasn't certain.

Throughout the year, when I have told friends about this thing I'm doing, sometimes they've said, *I'm going to try that for myself.* Others have said that it sounded horrifying to speak to a stranger that way. When I think about this—this fear of speaking to strangers, to interrupt their lives, to be rejected by even offering to wish them good—I can understand their hesitation. But it reminds me of a night that I encountered two junkyard dogs—because that's just the way my story brain works.

This act of communicating, of connecting, of sharing common ground, isn't just limited to alien races in a galaxy far, far away. I had to do the same when I pulled up late one night to bring some papers to an older couple (I wasn't serving papers, you understand; I think they were real estate related), and the couple just happened to live in a nice little house inside a junkyard. Okay—maybe it was an automotive place or something. The fact was, it had lots of stuff, equipment, cars, and so forth, and a high chain-link fence. The gate had been open so I promptly pulled inside, parked, and got out of my car, walking toward the house. Then I noticed two shapes emerging from the distance at a high rate of speed. Rottweilers wearing steel spikes for collars, teeth bared, eyes glowing green. At least that's the way it seemed to me, and I thought for sure that death was imminent. (I know, I know, my husband says I have a flair for the dramatic. Might be the writer in me.) But at that moment I swear I thought, no, I knew these creatures meant to kill me. Think something like Edgar Allan Poe. Think the hounds of hell. I don't carry a gun, don't run real fast, and even if I had something to swing, I'm just not that strong to injure four hundred pounds of dog muscle trying to eat me. My only possible weapon—baby talk.

I immediately started baby talking to those frightening, snarling beasts. "Oh, you are just such pretty big babies. Oh yes, you are, you sure are. Let me just get a closer look at you." Now, in retrospect, I can only call that moment divinely inspired because these trained killers were wagging what was left of their tails so hard they couldn't even walk in a straight line. They escorted me right up the stairs on the porch, ushered me to the door, and spent the remainder of the time only trying to lick me to death. When I went back to the car, they followed me, tailless tails wagging all the way, craving more of what they so desperately wanted to hear. A little ridiculous love.

That's what this whole business is about, really. A little ridiculous love for a stranger you pass and may never see again. If we want to get really crazy, we might just share a few words because sometimes we are as scary to one another as those rottweilers were to me coming up fast out of the darkness that night. Sometimes, we just need to find the invisible thread, the common ground, and dare to speak. Because we're all in this thing—the number and minutes of our days—together, and the sooner we realize that, the better for all of us.

NOTIONS

**When you pray for anyone you tend to
modify your personal attitude toward him.**

—NORMAN VINCENT PEALE

Y OU REALLY CAN'T JUDGE A BOOK BY THE COVER. NOT A
person either. I've been praying for people long
enough now that you'd think I'd know that. But it isn't so.
Still, I glance, make assumptions, and approach them under
the cover of ignorance.

Some of us may have grown up realizing that the homeless, the innocent, the unprotected, and those seemingly
hopeless need prayers. What has been a great challenge or
discovery for me during this resolution has been bumping
into those who don't look like they need prayer so much.
The ones that don't look like they need anything at all that
I have to offer. We look at the person with the sports car,
the big ring, or just the people we see who seem to just have
it more together than we do. Who would never do some-

thing inane and embarrassing. In other words, people who would never do half the inane and embarrassing things I've done because they are more adept at the social graces. They appear well put together, like my Little Miss Perfection, and seem as if they just don't err in life.

I'm standing in the grocery aisle when I look up and notice a woman that falls into that category. She's sharply dressed, wearing diamonds, obviously well-to-do. I look over both shoulders, make sure the aisle is empty of anyone else, and walk toward her. I've gotten to the point that I really try to talk to the person that suddenly catches my eye, my spirit, my attention—whatever you want to call it—in a special way. But in this case I want to argue with that leading. *Wrong woman, I want to say. Way off track. Today your chooser is obviously broken.*

I don't always dress to impress. Okay—that's an under-statement. I may have my Cinderella nights at the ball and special occasions, but in general I'm in blue jeans—in fact, as I write this now, I'm wearing jeans with a white T-shirt. It's my standard uniform or something close to it. Besides, I'm a woman who hates to shop for clothes. The woman I've chosen is obviously someone who has shopped for years with a discerning eye. I could swear she checks my shoes out and gives me the once-over as I approach her. I start by tell-ing her I'm a writer. An author of Southern fiction. I swear I may have even slipped in that I'm critically acclaimed because that ended up on a bio somewhere and it stuck like glue and has been used on every bio since then. Like that would add more credence to my prayers. For the record—it doesn't. I'm trying to make up for the fact that no doubt I'm wearing some three-dollar shirt I grabbed on the go and wished for the best.

She tells me her name is Peggy, and fifteen minutes later we're still talking about where she lives and the fact that she just relocated from a job in Texas. Then she asks would I please say special prayers for her grandson because there have been some situations there. Things aren't so good in that area. "We're having some trouble."

It reminds me once again that it's not what you're wearing or the name on the tag but what's on the inside that matters. We all have something to offer, no matter what our clothes, no matter what our station or title is. Just a little whisper of a prayer is all it takes.

Weeks later the strangest of things happens: I drive to a completely different area of Nashville in the middle of the day to shop for a gift for someone. I'm walking through this store and look up and there is Miss Peggy. I do a double take and so does she.

"Hey, I know you."

"You sure do," I tell her.

Basically, we pass one another with our standard Southern, "Have a good one." Not much conversation. An hour later I'm finding my way out of the store when I hear her call me.

"River Jordan, hey, River Jordan." I turn and she is waving me over to the linen department. "I want you to meet someone."

She introduces me to the woman behind the counter and explains to her that I'm a *writer*. A *novelist*. We exchange our "nice to meet you's" and then she is off to search for something at Peggy's request. As soon as the saleslady is out of ear range, Peggy tells me, "And that other situation I told you about, well, it's actually getting better. Things are turning around." I know she's referring to her grandson. And I know she's referring to the prayer.

"Good. I'm so glad to hear it." I tell her I'll see her sometime back in our neck of the woods.

I don't know how these occurrences happen—odd crossing in the city by people I've met in entirely other places, but I'm so glad that they do.

Dr. Mother

**He loves each one of us like there
is only one of us to love.**

—MAX LUCADO

I APPROACH A WOMAN WAITING IN THE DENTIST'S OFFICE
lobby. I am just finished with my appointment—just
a check-up and cleaning—when I see her. She is country
beautiful. By that I mean—well, just that. She is someone
straight out of a milk commercial. She's wholesome. A face
that could launch a million bags of flour, the kind you use
to make biscuits like nobody's business. A yellow cotton
dress that falls below her knees, white sneakers, a bun of
pure white, silken hair pulled on top of her head. The more
I think about it, she is exactly like my character Velma True
in the novel *Saints in Limbo*. Very much someone who you'd
expect to find rocking in a porch swing with a sweet face
and that pure white hair. Exactly the way I saw Velma in my
mind's eye when I was writing.

I'm about to discover she is absolutely nothing like that. I ask her name and she gallantly introduces herself. I use that word seriously because this woman is full of gusto, and a kind of fearless confidence. "Dr. Jones," she tells me. "But retired now that I'm eighty-seven."

Power. That's what she has, I decide. I take a small step back. "Why, do you recognize me?" she asks. "Have I doctored you?" She takes a closer look at me. "I've doctored lots of folks."

"No, ma'am," I say. "I'm not from around here. It's that I'm just, it's just that . . ." I falter just a little. "Pray for people, that's what I do. Not in the open, mind you," I shake my head back and forth in a no, no kind of way. "But I do pray." She eyes me up and down. We are alone in this waiting room and I'm thinking it's a good thing for me. If for any reason I'm going to get a lecture, I'd rather go without a witness. But that's not what happens. "It's a simple resolution," I tell her. "Or at least it started that way."

Her name is Mary Jones and she begins to give me what I would call an education. About Tennessee and times gone past. Cold winters and babies, and about her patients in general. I am amazed by her. Everything about her. The only woman I've ever met with this kind of confidence is my mother. She amazes me and scares me some, too.

"So before I go," I ask as is my habit, "anything special you'd like me to pray for later?" I'm leaning on my "later." Like always. Witnesses or no, I prefer to take my prayers to the closet.

She looks down for a moment, wiggles her toes in those white sneakers, and I shake my head again thinking how much she reminds me of my character Velma on the outside.

"I'm having trouble with my daughter," she says. "She won't listen to anything I tell her."

"Your daughter?"

She nods her head and then gets a little riled up, obviously remembering some recent conversation. "She's sixtynine and thinks she knows everything. I tell her and tell her but she won't listen to a word I say." She stomps down on the last word. "Nothing, I tell you. I get so tired of trying to tell her."

"Kids," I say. "What are you going to do? My sons don't listen to me either."

She nods her head. "Isn't it the truth."

We talk a little about children and mothering. I tell her my mother tried to tell me things many years ago but it took me a very long time to catch up with the wisdom, to admit that she had been right. I also tell her that tug-of-war is a mother-daughter game; it's just that way sometimes, to go round with one another once in a while and disagree.

Then the nurse opens the door and calls her name. "Nice meeting you," she says as she rises to follow her. Then she is quickly off around the corner, where I hear her reminding them of exactly who she is lest they have forgotten. She would terrify me if she was my mother, but she isn't. Just a stranger, Dr. Mary, mother of Polly, warrior of something. I sure would want her on my side.

I open the door and step into the sunshine and take the long way home thinking of country doctors, and women who know their place, of mothers and daughters and a hundred other things, but all of them are related to my special lady in a country yellow dress and how much I wish I were more like her. Could that be another thing worth picking up along the way? Could I be inspired to be more joyful like the housekeeper in the mountains, more helpful like the man from the back roads, more confident like Dr. Mary? Could the people that I encounter each somehow teach me something by their lives and through their memories?

PEARLS OF WISDOM

**But miracles don't c-c-c-cause belief—real miracles
don't m-m-m-make faith out of thin air; you have to
already have faith in order to believe in real miracles.**

—JOHN IRVING, *A PRAYER FOR OWEN MEANY*

I'M WITH MY HUSBAND AT THE DOCTOR'S OFFICE WHERE HE'S having some tests done. I find him almost superhuman, this husband of mine. He's an athlete. A real one who can ride his bike a hundred miles or more and in my mind leap tall buildings in a single bound. We are planning to celebrate our fifteen-year anniversary soon and it amazes me still. I am a bookworm. A bike to me represents something that gets in the way of being able to focus clearly on the words. An unnecessary distraction. Still, he shows me a different side of life. I've hiked with him up twelve thousand miles through bear country where he carried all the supplies on his back and I carried lip gloss. We slept on the roof of our van in an alligator swamp with him daring a gator to come near us. We traveled across Europe with nothing but back-packs. He is fearless. I am faithful. We make a good team.

But now we are in one of the places that, truth be told, he does fear—the doctor's office. He hates being sick more than any person I have ever known. He detests weakness in himself. He abhors the idea of not being able to pursue life full of the kind of gusto that only he can muster. Tests, and more frustrating tests, for an unknown muscle condition have brought us to the office, in the waiting room, where he is pensive and short of words.

Somehow the two of us got around to talking about his home state of Pennsylvania, perhaps discussing sports, or news from friends from afar. An older gentleman overhears and approaches us, tells us he is from Pennsylvania. Nor-mally, my husband being the much more outgoing of the two of us would have taken off on that conversation, but he is tight-lipped and short-spoken. But I've been introducing myself to a stranger every day and I really like old people. They're a wonder to me. They captivate me with their sto-ries. And the fact that they are so easy in their skin. When you are eighty-two years old, you know a thing or two. One of them is that you really know yourself and that's what strikes me as this man steps up and begins to talk about Philly and the old neighborhood. I pipe in and ask a few questions, then he grabs my hand and says, "Come meet my wife, Pearl. She's eighty-six now. I'm eighty-two, you know. I married an older woman!"

He leads me across the waiting room but my husband remains behind, stationary and quiet. "Pearl," Gus exclaims, "this is River."

Pearl puts out her hand with skin as thin as lace, and holds mine steady instead of shaking it. Then she squeezes my palm and says, "Stay out of the sun!" These are her first words to me.

"Funny you should say that." I lean in a little. "Because I was just seriously considering getting a tan."

Now, you may think this is no big deal. People are getting in tanning beds everywhere, spraying on color, getting that golden glow. But it is different with me. I grew up on the Gulf Coast, and a main part of those years was being the color of brown sugar. It was the days when suntan lotion hit a whole new level of bronzing power. The days of suntan lotions that wore warning labels on them saying you had to have a dark tan before you even thought about using that product. To say I might have accelerated the damage by using that great baking mixture of baby oil and iodine is an understatement. But I must admit, I had a perpetual golden glow once upon a time.

Never mind all that now. I've carved out years behind the keyboard and out of the light. I've covered up, slathered on SPF 45 sunscreen, and sat in the shade. But two days before I ran into Gus and Pearl, I had decided that I was sick of being pasty olive. I didn't want a fake tan or a spray-on anything. I wanted to be a lizard on the sand like the old days. So what if

I had moved to Tennessee; I'd sunbathe on Old Rocky Top if I needed to. I wanted to be the color I was my senior year in high school. The one that made the American Indian heritage side of me a little more pronounced and not the white legs of my Irish ancestors. I was going to turn a deaf ear to warnings of all kinds and bake myself to a glorious, golden brown.

"Stay out of the sun," Pearl says again. "It'll hurt you."

Maybe I didn't mention that I'd had a few teeny, tiny spots removed that showed they were up to something or moving toward something a person doesn't want to have. "I hear you, Pearl. Funny you should say that. I was about to start working on that in a big way."

"Nope. Wear that lotion. And a big hat. Get you a big hat."

"Yes, Pearl, lotion and a big hat."

Then I visited with them a little bit. Found out that a son of theirs had driven them to Nashville to see the doctor. And I decided that today I would pray for two strangers because Gus and Pearl came as a package deal. You couldn't have one without the other. I wanted to just go home with them. To sit at their kitchen table and have them tell me stories till the cows came home. But there would be none of that as the nurse called my husband's name and it was time for me to go.

I didn't see them on our way out, but I decided to bag my new dreams of tanning for hours without protection and soaking up rays with abandon. It was short-lived and most likely right on the cusp of Pearl's warning for good reason. What if that's just the way things were meant to work? That strangers could bear us strange gifts, gifts that might remain unopened if we never make contact with one another.

What if the unseen things, the wonder, advice, leading we needed was just out of reach, resting in the palm of a stranger's hand, waiting for us to touch them?

FRIENDS AND FEELING LONESOME

**Prayer does not fit us for the greater work;
prayer is the greater work.**

—OSWALD CHAMBERS

Although I've traveled and lived in many places, I'm
originally from the Gulf Coast, a place my husband
and I jointly called home for years. A northern area of Florida that's—at least in my memory—still a backwoods fishing village, a pristine place with Mom and Pop restaurants
scattered along the beach and a place called Long Beach that
offered a few kiddie rides, corn dogs, and cotton candy.

Now, condos fill the air. Restaurants aren't scattered anymore but are almost stacked on one another, and spring
breakers have discovered the huge nightclubs that crushed
sand dunes by the dozens. It has become a different kind of
place than the one I grew up in. Still, when I go "home," the

smell of saltwater in the air, the slapping rhythm of the palm trees, the few nights where we watch shooting stars from the beach, a little of that old magic finds its way to the surface.

The only problem with a visit home is that instead of becoming a respite—time to recover from deadlines—it becomes work itself. We're blessed that these visits are filled with family and old friends, but finding the time to visit all of them is impossible. The clock hands tick, the few days rush by so quickly, and still I haven't spent enough time with almost anyone and I've missed or left out a multitude. There's always pressure to visit and see more old friends than I can possibly fit in, to the point that going home is never restful. There's just not enough of me left to go around.

I'm on one of these trips home and I'm on a late-night errand, hurrying through the store aisles. It's almost closing time and I'm trying to get all the things we need, plus special things our mothers like, when I rush past a man in the frozen food aisle. Abruptly my speed slows to half. He's wearing a white jacket and stocking the shelves. I'm walking one slow step at a time, testing that old, familiar feeling. Then I turn around and plod my way back, my entire "hurry up" all gone.

"Hey, there . . ." He's wearing a name tag so that when he stands up from the freezer, I can read it. "Ron. I have this resolution that I say a special prayer for someone every day, and you're my someone. Just want you to know . . . special prayers . . . special blessings. So that's it. Take care."

I'm turning to go, to get my rush back, to pick up where I left off on my list, but then I notice he's just standing there, has put his hands in the front pockets of his coat.

"Thanks 'cause I sure do need it."

"Hey, Ron, me, too. We all need it." Walking backward now, I work my way around the freezer section and almost into the next aisle. Yogurt, I'm thinking, maybe I should get some yogurt.

"Where do you go to church?"

I stop walking. This isn't one of those "walk by, pray for a stranger" events. I fold my list, put it in my pocket, walk back toward him, and cross my arms to get comfortable.

"Just visiting, Ron. We don't live here anymore."

"Oh?"

"Yep, up in Nashville now."

"I been thinking about going back to church. I used to go to a church here. Been thinking of going back there or maybe visiting some other churches."

He's a big man. The kind of man that might have played football, the kind that probably gets asked to help people move a lot. The kind of man that looks like maybe he would have been a good butcher, like he could lift half a cow with one hand or something. But in spite of that, tonight he just looks tired, and a little lonely, like a man who seems to be tired from more than working the late shift. Like a man that could use a friend or two. In this case, I don't mean me just slowing down. I mean a friend, family, and a network

of people that will catch him if he falls. Will listen to his
dried-up dreams until they can regain new life.

I tell him about a church nearby, one a friend attends.
"They seem really friendly over there. It's a casual place,
jeans and such. You don't have to dress up to fit in." He
doesn't strike me as a man that has more than one suit and
that would be the one that he only wears for a funeral.

"I've heard about that place, I think. Maybe I'll go check
it out this Sunday."

"Take care, Ron."

"I will. And you be careful going back to Nashville."

I pull the list out, finish my shopping, then step out into
that warm Gulf Coast night thinking of my problem of too
much family and too many friends. And I realize that as
messy as it may be, there's really no such thing as too many
friends. But there is surely something as too few.

SAINTLESS MOMENTS

No words exchanged, no time to exchange.

—DAVE MATTHEWS

GOD, SHE MUST HAVE BEEN SO LONELY. THAT'S WHAT I REALize a little too late. After I have bulldozed my way through the checkout line with little to no patience. You know, I am a friendly person given the right occasion. That occasion being something nearing a perfect summer afternoon where all of my deadlines have been met, my errands run, my life seemingly at a standstill. Given those circumstances, and say I bumped into you down the road at the country store, well, we might strike up a conversation about how hot it was or how blue the sky, then we might just carry it right out to the store porch, where those rocking chairs are waiting. We could rock an hour, maybe two, and share some stories. I could be that way for you—I swear I could. Only that day is like a strange rising Egyptian moon, like Halley's Comet. Those moments are so rare that maybe I just need to stand flat-footed in my determination, steely-eyed and unrepentant in that I will take time to be human. That I will somehow become all the things I wasn't yesterday. After praying for strangers for months on end. After making contact, getting stories, seeing the difference it makes in others and in me. But instead it happened this way.

I'm just trying to get through an express lane checkout because I am in an express lane state of mind, but the woman in front of me should have taken a different lane. A very, very long, slow lane. It's not the amount of items that she has; it's the fact that she wants to talk about every single item with the cashier. Then she's talking about other personal stuff, but I'm not really listening because I'm actually fighting the urge to tap my nails in that click, click, click way that says only one thing: *I'm waiting.*

Then she pays, but she doesn't *leave.* The cashier has *finally* started to ring my items up.

"Having a good day, ma'am?" he asks me as he pulls an item across the scanner.

"Oh, yes, great day. Very fine day." I say this in one half a breath and want to grab some of the items and scan them for him saying, "Like this—zoom, zoom, zoom. Times awaiting." But I make nice, stand still, force my hands to my sides, and smile.

The woman is still standing there and then she leans over to the cashier, distracting him, and says, "And I'd like to buy some stamps."

Stamps? Stamps?! This isn't a post office, or at least go to Customer Service—over there. Get out of line. Stop distracting the cashier!

Okay, I don't say any of this either. The cashier tells her, "Sure, no problem, after I finish this order," and of course, I'm thinking that at this rate he is never going to finish ringing me up.

Then the woman leans over closer, begins to inspect my items that are not being bagged yet. "Submarine sandwiches? Is that what you have there?"

"Yes, ma'am," I say.

"I didn't know they made submarine sandwiches."

Now, what I'm thinking at this point is two things at exactly the same time: (1) This woman must be my stranger for the day, and (2) I've got to get out of here!

"They make great subs here, they really do." The cashier offers that they are better than a leading chain. I tell her I agree.

"Well, now I hear about this. I'm just going to have to check those out."

I'm grabbing my bags like a hurricane in a knot and telling her, "Yes, ma'am, you should do that. Take care of yourself," I say as I brush past her.

She says, "You, too." But I'm already halfway to the door.

It's not until I've completed another hour of errands, until I'm driving home trying to get back into the office and get another hour of writing in for the day, that it suddenly hits me. Those seven words just like that: God, she must have been so lonely.

I didn't tell her that she was my stranger, but I bet it would have put a new light in her eyes. To be singled out, to be thought special. The least I could have done was engage her in a conversation while the young man scanned my items. I could have said something, anything, about the weather, airplanes, and the price of eggs. I could have looked in her bags, or asked her if she wanted to meet me there and split a sub one day for lunch, where we could talk for forty minutes. Yes, I could have done any number of those things. From the smallest to the greatest, but all I did was hold my breath until I could get away. Because the ugly truth is it's so much easier to put her on my "prayer list" than to give her five minutes of my undivided attention.

This resolution has provided me with an instrument I didn't ask for—a way to see inside my soul on days when I'm as saintless and selfish as they come.

Yes, I prayed for this woman, I really did. I prayed she'd meet a better person than I am. Someone with the patience to listen, and would take the time to really hear. And I prayed that I could be a person like that more often than not.

TEARS OF TROUBLE

Good things happen when you meet strangers.

—YO-YO MA

MY HUSBAND IS SCHEDULED FOR OUTPATIENT SURGERY, still trying to discover what's troubling his muscles. He looks healthy as a horse. No, healthier. But recent muscle spasms have sent him seeking sage advice. He's a frustrated bear, not a very good patient, and not a man given to taking pills much less undergoing any kind of surgery. I'm hanging out with him before surgery both for moral support and to protect those he comes in contact with. *A hospital*, I'm thinking. *Lots of sick people here.* Finding a stranger in this room full of people waiting for surgery will have to be one of the easiest days I've ever had choosing someone to pray for.

My eyes have scanned the area. It's a surgical waiting room in a major Nashville hospital. There are people of every background, race, and experience. A veritable melting pot of those who might need prayer, and given their current circumstances, not only need it but actually appreciate it. A couple holding hands in the waiting room. A mother with two small children trying to keep them occupied. This menagerie of people flipping through used magazines never lingering long enough on a page for the words to actually register. The television is turned to a daytime soap, but no one is really following the story line. And my husband and I are sitting among them. We were asked to arrive at this time, but the surgery isn't scheduled for a few hours.

My husband asks, "Why? Why do they schedule it so you have to wait so long?"

I don't have an answer to his question. I only know it certainly gives the anxiety a chance to build for everyone. The general worry about every little detail. I search for the closest restroom and end up wandering the halls. All hospitals are a maze to me. Blind, medicinal corridors that lead to other corridors that look identical to those I've just turned down.

In the women's room, I'm standing behind a young woman, waiting to wash my hands, and thinking—*There's my person.* A part of my brain argues with my heart. The part that always thinks telling people is a stupid inconvenience anyway. *She's not sick,* it says. *Look, she even has some kind of name tag. She works here. Wrong person.* My spirit overrules my brain.

"Excuse me, but may I ask your name?" The young lady

turns. Young, I'd say. Maybe thirty. Young enough. She's brushing tears away from her cheeks when she turns to face me. I hadn't noticed that she was crying. At least a part of me hadn't noticed. But maybe that other part of me had.

"Felicia," she says softly. She really is wearing a name tag. She doesn't look sick. She looks beautiful but sad.

"Today you're my stranger." So the conversation begins. She needs a listening ear, a few kind words, a hug. And all three of those things take only a few minutes. It's a brief slice of time. No one else walks into the restroom and interferes with our few private moments. I tell her good-bye and blessings abounding. Then I find my husband still waiting impatiently.

"Want to hear a story?" To put that question into context, this is something my husband hears a lot. "Do you want to hear a story?" could translate to: *I've really been thinking about quantum physics lately, and even though I can't understand algebra, I think I get this string theory thing.* To which he might reply, as in days past: *You are making my brain hurt.* Or it could mean, quite literally, that if you want to hear a story, I will whip out George Garrett's *Bad Man Blues* or Jack London's *Call of the Wild* or Haven Kimmel's *A Girl Named Zippy* and I will read to you until you turn blue. With fifteen years of these kinds of responses, he has learned to qualify the question.

"Is it about your prayer person?"

"Yes."

"Okay, then."

So I proceed to tell him about the girl in front of the sink.

"And you didn't know she was crying?"

"Not until she turned around."

"I'm telling you, you have to write these stories down."

He says that all the time. Or at least every time I tell him a story. I don't tell him all of them, but there are days when my story cup runneth over, so to speak. Days where I'm simply amazed by little things and small coincidences. Like the fact that I might ask someone their name only to discover that they'd been crying at that precise moment.

Yes, it amazes me. It doesn't happen that way all the time, not every day, but when it does, I realize that there is a part of me—a still, silent part of me—listening with my spirit to a cry my ears would never hear.

ETERNAL SISTERS

He who prays for his neighbors
will be heard for himself.

—THE TALMUD

I HAVE JOURNALS ABOUT PRAYING FOR STRANGERS. I HAVE journals and notepads, names scribbled on napkins, receipts, paper menus, names—so many names. Jack, Jerry, Miriah, Courtney, and the list goes on and on. Old names, family names, Southern sharecropping names and brave new names that some creative mother fashioned to fit her unique child.

Only a few days ago I was questioning why I even ask people their names. Why do I always start out with this question? See, I'm not normally one who asks people their names, I'm the shy five-year-old, the one who could barely put her head up and her hand out, the one who at twelve would have preferred to be invisible, the one who cried as a grown woman because her picture was being put in the

newspaper with a book review. Oh, don't get me wrong: I
have worked jobs that required me to smile, put out my
hand, and sell a commercial, but . . . that was work. My
own time was my private shell, my life, and hands off, not
hands out. But just today I asked someone her name and it
struck me. I asked a woman her name in the vet's office—
just because I knew she had one, and she deserved not to be
one of the nameless faces serving me. Regardless of whether
or not I was paying for those dog shots, it occurred to me
that I hadn't paid a price for her anonymity. I have learned
something elemental about connecting and communicating with the human race. Everyone has a name—and they
long to be seen, to be heard, and to be acknowledged for
more than just being another cashier at the counter, driver
behind the wheel, waitress, ticket taker with those little
informative tags on their shirts. Those names mean more to
me now. I've been asking names for many days. And finally
I'm beginning to hear, really hear, the answers.

I would encourage everyone I know to pray for a stranger
every day. There are benefits I've discovered in doing this
that surprised me. Those moments of the day where you
stop your brain from thinking about a thousand other
things, just become aware of those around you and begin
to sense that big blanket of human need out there, well, I
think it lowers blood pressure. I think it staves off ulcers
and panic attacks. I used to think opening yourself up to
the world was a dangerous thing, but there is healing in the

process. Maybe telling the person just isn't something you might feel comfortable doing, and I can certainly understand that, but that shouldn't keep someone from embarking on the adventure. Of course, without the telling, you don't get the story. You don't get the opportunity to make a connection with someone else right here and right now in your lifetime. The chance you take is that they might not want your prayers, and that's okay. No big worries if they don't, but trust me, this has not been my experience after praying for people daily for months. Everyone, no matter what their faith, their background, their race may be, is unified in their desire to be blessed.

The tricky part—something that might take a little getting used to—is that the person you pray for often defies natural selection. In other words, logic is out the window.

For instance, that man over there dragging his oxygen tank around with him, barely able to breathe? Surely this is an easy one, right? One of those things we might call a no-brainer. I don't have to go on some kind of spiritual scavenger hunt to find the right choice. Here's a man barely breathing, a little angry, and dragging an oxygen tank behind him. It's so obvious.

But then a woman gets out of a car right behind him, and she immediately captures my attention. She's coming into the post office as I'm getting ready to leave, and before I know it, I'm standing next to the man with the breathing machine but fully concentrating on this woman.

She looks fine. Really. She's an attractive, middle-aged woman who just got out of a nice car. *Look*, I tell myself, *her life is probably a piece of cake and she doesn't even need prayer but the guy next to me is in a pretty rough spot. Still . . .*

She asks me if the post office is already closed.

"Not yet," I say. "You have exactly two minutes." I step back inside the door, contemplating her instead of talking to the man at the postage machine or giving up on the whole prayer thing for the day and rushing to my car. On my left the man with the oxygen tank is trying to do something at the self-service table. He begins to stamp envelopes. He's breathing heavily through a tube and he's obviously a little ticked, and who could blame him in that condition? I begin to argue with myself. *This has to be my person. This is a man that needs prayer.* I'm about to step up and say something to him, but today he's not my stranger. I look back at the woman. It's her. I don't know why it is, but I do know it is her. I wait for her at the exit, hold the door open for her as she walks outside, and say, "Just one minute, please." Then I explain my mission and myself. She clasps her hands in front of her chest and says, "You are an answer to my prayer. You are just confirmation to me." Her accent sounds Filipino. "I am on my way tonight to a special Mass in Kentucky. I've been having some serious health problems," she goes on. "This past year, it has been"—and she searches for words—"so heavy." I tell her that I will pray for her. That I will pray for her health and for many blessings and for a better year. She hugs me and asks my name. She says she will pray for me, too, and asks what I would like prayer for. Only one thing comes to mind but then it's always foremost on my mind. I tell her my sons are deployed and both in war zones and that I'd like prayer for them.

"What are their names?" She is walking with me now to my car.

"Nicholas and Christopher."

She stops in the parking lot and clasps her hands together. "Oh, my—you are giving me chills. Those were the names I chose for my sons, but I had only girls."

Maria is reluctant to leave me. We walk across the darkening parking lot. She follows me to my car and hugs me again and declares, "If we never see each other again, our spirits will always know each other. We will always know in here," and she points to her heart. She hugs me again and then she is gone.

Am I learning to trust myself? No. But I'm learning to trust something greater than myself. The offering of a prayer to heal and mend people is like the smallest offering in a sea, like one gold coin dropped in a plate. But my willingness to do this, my faith to do this, makes things right in spite of myself. There are no right people or wrong people to pray for. We all need it. This big old beautiful, tired, worn world is full of souls hungry for prayer. But some power pulls me in the right direction daily, it shows me the special people in my path, people who have been asking for prayer, for a sign, for a good word to keep them going.

And now I have the comfort of Maria's words. I know on odd days, and strange nights, perhaps when I need it most or feel I can't go on, some small but powerful lady named Maria will be sending a special prayer in my direction because now she knows me by name.

FACES IN THE DARK

Prayer is not asking for what you think you want, but
asking to be changed in ways you can't imagine.

—KATHLEEN NORRIS

WHAT IS IT ABOUT A FACE THAT WE GLIMPSE IN PASSING
that so captures our attention? Is it that possibility,
that flash of almost recognition of, do I know you? Yesterday,
as I was sitting in my car in traffic, a man called out to me as
he turned the corner. He raised his hand as if to say, *Wait, I know
you.* Or maybe it was, *Wait, I need you.* Then the light changed.
The car behind me honked and I needed to keep driving. I
wasn't quite sure who that man was, but when I lie down at
night, his face is there, just in the outline of the dark, invading
that quiet space before dreams come. And he is laying out his
needs before me. I don't know what they are—only that they
are. So I sift some of my needs out of the way, try to make
room for that man's eyes, his old scraggly beard, try to push
my wants out of the way so I can lift his face up to God.

Now, no doubt, God knows him. Knows what he has need of and want of more than I do. But I'm following this path of believing that one person's prayers in this big world can shake up something invisible in the spirit realm. That we set forth on due course a better future for those we encounter and remember. I'm thinking that's part of the way things were set into motion at the beginning of time. With each passing day, I'm becoming more certain of it.

Recently, I've been reading Thomas Merton, a monk and writer of notable prestige and someone I've long envied. Not for the accolades he received for his writing, which would make obvious sense, but for his solitude, his aloneness with nature and with God. But this year is teaching me something about myself I never knew. I wasn't meant to be alone. That very thing that I've craved and longed for, believed maybe I was destined for, and have not fulfilled, was never my calling. My destiny was that elderly face in the car window, the child on the bus, the woman on the passing train. I was born to lose myself in humanity and that's no easy thing for me.

I've always wondered at Jesus. I can get the part of him that is able to stay peaceful and calm in the middle of a raging storm on the sea. But it's his magnificence to stay calm and peaceful in the sea of humanity that has left me in awe and wonder. Is this what it means to love? To continue moving among people, all people, with an open face. I've always found people rather threatening. Not in a fearful, hide-me-quick kind of way, but in their noise, their needs, their messy unforgiveness. But now I'm remembering the face of the young girl I passed walking through the woods, her arm in a sling, her eyes looking haunted by something I couldn't see. She was with a few other girls, or I would have spoken to her, but now I'm sorry that I didn't do more than have that moment of brief eye contact. The one where I took in the weary, wary soul. Now she's another nameless face on my list that hasn't found its way to my life by chance.

The man on the street, the face on the train, the girl in the woods—there must be reasons for crossing one another's paths, a reason for this crisscross life of ours. If those moments of human interaction became personal, became prayerful, if the connection became universal, I wonder what would happen.

Now my life is full of flashes of faces of the people along my path. I now write these encounters down on scraps of paper. I have scratched down the Birdhouse Man, the Grocery Boy, the Airplane Girl. It goes on like that. Notes I pull out of pockets and purses, from suitcases, and laptop bags. They spill out from everywhere. They're like little bread crumbs, leaving illuminated trails of where I've been this year, of the people I've encountered along the way, and also a memory of their need or smile or situation.

I transfer names to my journals, transfer words from journals to the laptop, in my attempt to record this journey as much as living it. But the stories always stop me from more typing. The journals lie around half-filled, the laptop even less so. I stare out the window and think of people that have crossed my path. Mostly I remember their faces—again in no particular order. They just come calling, seemingly at will. What astounds me is how much I remember them in detail. How they really are snapshots that have been etched just like that—bam, like the old gunpowder used to ignite a camera. In that same manner, these strangers are frozen in time in my mind. The way they were standing just so, the tilt of a head or outstretched hand to shake mine. Captured. Contained. Forever. This is another one of the things that I didn't bargain for at the first of the year. One of the many, many things that I didn't have a clue about. That I'd have this scrapbook of faces frozen in time. But now I do. Now I've got them. Guess I'll have to just pray for them forever.

SMALL TOWN BLUES

There is nothing that makes us love a man
so much as praying for him.

—WILLIAM LAW

I'VE PASSED THROUGH HUNDREDS OF SMALL TOWNS IN MY life. Was raised in the proximity of so many more, have passed through a hundred on the journey of my life, trying to get to the next place on down the road.

Not so long ago I pulled up and parked at that cabin in the woods to write. The closest place to travel to for the most basic of supplies is not actually an official town, but a place in the middle of the woods, a spot on the map. A small little grocery, a gas station, a video store, and a dollar store make up the busy commerce section at the traffic light. My guess is children are bused to the closest city for school. I know these places. My mother and father grew up in these places, and I spent my summers there. The backwoods are full of beautiful people, full of funny stories and hearts of gold, but just passing through, you might not notice these things. What you might notice is what seems to be missing—that is, a viable way to make a decent living.

I wander into the dollar store looking for something to kill scorpions and hairy spiders the size of rats. "Bug killer," I kept asking the girl behind the counter, "not bug spray for mosquitoes. I need scorpion killer."

"Scorpion killer? Don't know that we have anything like that. Got ant killer and maybe roach killer but they may be it."

"Just point me to the poison," I tell her. At this point I'd just about use straight DDT to try to take the things out, offing myself in the process. Just think Bill Murray's character in *Caddyshack* with that cute little rodent. Scorpions are not cute. They are the epitome of all things not cute. I so very much want to kill them all.

The girl is right. There is nothing with any kind of skull and crossbones warning that will kill anything close to a scorpion. I try to make myself feel better by buying a collection of B-rated old black-and-white movies on a DVD— four movies on sale for the price of $3.99. Surely even a writer without cable or television should watch a late-night flick to help her not think too hard about sleeping in the middle of a room full of spiders and scorpions on a life-raft bed with her shoes on? I would think so.

When I approach the young girl to check out, this time I notice she is about six months pregnant—and that she is my stranger. She looks so tired. The kind of tired that goes beyond being pregnant and standing on your feet all day, bagging bug spray and canned goods and cleaning supplies. There's a soul-weary expression on her face, and I start to tell her that she's my stranger while she's bagging my items, but then a woman gets in line behind me. Then another person gets in line behind her. I'm sure no one wants me to be slowing things down by telling a story. But I still ask the cashier her name.

"Sharon." She looks at me a little closer, trying to determine if we know one another.

So I share with her about my resolution, about the fact that she is my stranger, that in the middle of everything else and trying to kill scorpions, I'll be praying for her to have great blessings in her life. And for her baby, too.

I wish I could take a snapshot of the smile that crosses her face, of the light that appears from nowhere, of the soft thank-you she whispers to me. It's amazing how little it takes, the pause of a moment within the breath of a moment, to make a difference to someone.

When I leave, I really do pray for Sharon, if you would call it a prayer. Some people might call it more of an intercession. Me knocking on heaven's door, if you will, kind of saying, "C'mon, what're her chances here? She needs things and that baby needs things and most of all she needs a future."

Sharon suddenly isn't a nameless cashier in a quick stop

in the backwoods of my life. She isn't just a walk-on character that rang me up, bagged my stuff, and disappeared from
the pages of my life like a three-cent character. Suddenly
Sharon, her baby, and the memory of the both of them are
an integrated part of my puzzle. I can handle that.

BEHIND THE MASK

**If thou shouldst never see my face again,
pray for my soul.**

—ALFRED, LORD TENNYSON

I'M HAVING ANOTHER ONE OF MY DAYS. THE KIND WHERE I SAY I'm busy, busy, busy. One where there is no time for strangers in my life, which is pretty ironic considering that unless I am away on a writer's retreat, strangers are a part of my world every day. But it's a day where I think I am literally too busy to slow down and have a simple conversation with someone I don't know. Never mind that I usually travel with earphones or plugged into my cell phone, stopping to text someone about something work related in between appointments. None of that counts because those things I've brought into my world. Have I told you I'm the type of person that will wear earphones in a crowded place even if I'm not listening to anything just so strangers will not bother me? Okay—that was before this resolution, but seriously, have you heard of such a thing? I have no ear-phones today. I have an errand list, a grocery list, and a rush to get it all done before I rush home again.

I'm at one of my favorite high-service grocery stores. "Can I carry that for you?" "Help you find something?" "Questions about anything?" And I've made it through the aisles and down my list in record time. If I've forgotten anything at all, there will be no going back. I'm headed for the door and my finish line. A young lady offers to push my groceries to the car and I say, "Sure, go ahead," always thinking people just crave fresh air and a moment of respite from fluorescent lights.

So here we go. I'm watching my watch, the girl pushing the cart is watching the door, and we've almost made it out when a grocery employee says, "Thanks for shopping with us. Hope you have a nice day."

I immediately turn to the girl pushing the cart and say just one minute because in all my hurry up and go mode, I've learned that in the snap of a finger, at least _almost every time,_ I'll drop everything I'm doing to talk to one specific person who captures my attention in a unique way.

"What's your name, because today—you're my stranger."

There was just a little more explanation there but that sums it up.

"Thank you, thank you so much. You have no idea how much that means to me." And as I am saying my _Well, good, and you don't have to thank me_ and so on—the girl bursts into tears. I turn to the young lady pushing the cart for me and say, "It's okay, I've got this one," so that she won't be frozen in what has already become an awkward moment for her as her coworker stands there suddenly crying.

"Can you walk with me to my car?" I ask the stranger, figuring now maybe she's the one that could use a little fresh air and someone to hear her story.

Here's the thing that gets me most—really, really gets to me. Some years ago Billy Joel came out with a song titled "The Stranger," the one that illuminated the fact that everyone was wearing a mask for others to see, not their real faces, not what was really going on behind those eyes. It was a catchy tune. What it reminds me of now, with this girl pouring out her story between tears, is that we're all wearing our stranger faces. Most of us are getting up in the morning and plastering them on tight, never really removing them at all until we are certain the lights are out, that the theater's empty, and that we alone remain there acting out our lives. We are constantly, continuously performing. No wonder we are so exhausted and taking Prozac, Xanax, and everything in between.

"My dad is sick and it's been so hard," Rachel says, then she goes on, "and I have to work this schedule, but I miss my church family. You know, they were really helping me through this thing with Dad, but now I'm working. But I'm glad to have a job, I mean don't get me wrong, I really like my work and I know lots of people don't have work so I'm lucky, you know? It's just that . . ."

"I know," I tell her, "I know." When I am in the middle of complaining about book deadlines or editing or—I'm so thankful to have these complaints really, it's just that . . .

And I guess the "just that" is that we are human after all. That at a moment's notice, with the touch of a human kindness, the prayer of a stranger, we can crumble and lose all our carefully planned reserves. That mask can fall off so fast we are left naked-faced and scrambling for cover. But as other grocery patrons and kind helpers are strolling to their cars, I'm listening to Rachel, patting her shoulder, telling her it'll be all right. And yes, praying that maybe her schedule can change, or that those special "church family" members will think of her and search her out when it is her day off, outside the boundaries of their familiar schedules and routines. That the people she calls family show up when they're needed, not just when it's convenient. And then I remind myself of these words as they apply to my own life, to those around me.

I hope that Rachel being stopped and pulled out of her life, that spending a few minutes in a parking lot talking about her troubles, has helped her. I hope that it makes a difference, or that maybe that coworker can ask her about those tears later in a nice way so that a few more walls are broken down. Those stranger faces can really handicap us all. I mean, really, who are we trying so hard to hide from?

MAKING TIME

**When the fire of prayer goes out,
the barrenness of busyness takes over.**

—GEORGE CAREY

How do you know who to pray for? How do you decide? People continue to ask me as my resolution progresses. I don't know how to answer that exactly. Sometimes I get a gut feeling. Sometimes not so much. I don't think it matters so much in the long run. I think everyone needs some kind of prayer. But, all that being said, if this searchlight in my spirit is on, looking for a specific person, it has a habit of causing me to be more aware of those around me all day long. Not that I'm looking for that. Oh, but I guess I am; somewhere in my mind, I'm obviously wanting to force myself to stay a part of an intertwined life. Remain linked to others on the planet. And maybe that's because I know how much I could retreat into a private world and live out the rest of my existence there.

I'm on my way to a book affair, another signing. And when en route to these things, I rarely stop. I eat my tuna behind the wheel and just keep driving. When I must take a break, I pull into rest stops, not to rest but because they are the fastest way to get back on the road again.

Today, I'm in the rest stop bathroom when I sense that a woman is my stranger for the day. Well, I don't want to talk to a woman in the bathroom. Really, I just want to get back on the road and make good time. Regardless, I go outside and stand around the water fountain waiting for her to come out so that I can speak to her away from the sound of flushing toilets. When she exits, I hear her and she's noticeably humming. Humming to me is a happy noise. I hum when my husband goes deep-sea fishing and comes home with fresh snapper that he will have cleaned and on my plate in a matter of hours. It brings out the happy in me. My mother hums when she is decorating for Christmas because it's her favorite time of year.

When I hear this woman humming, I tell myself, *That's it—I'm back on the road. This woman doesn't even need prayer. She's humming, she's happy.*

I began walking to my car, she's walking to hers in the opposite direction, and before I can count to three, I turn around and am chasing her down. The turnaround chase-down has also become a part of my repertoire. It's as if I give my feet permission to run ahead of my mind, to say hello, to stop someone before part of my brain can override the impulse.

"Excuse me, what is your name?" It's my disarming question. When she tells me, I share the stranger story, tell her I'll be praying for her. Then she surprises me and grabs my hand and says, "Oh, please pray for me!"

I look to my left and right. It's a quiet rest stop, no one is walking near us, but I have to tell her, "Well, it's not something I normally do in public. I simply think about the person, you know? During the day, at night before I fall asleep." Then I make eye contact, real contact, the way maybe we should more often but don't take the risk. I see the pain in there behind all that humming. "Anything special that you need prayer for?"

She nods yes as tears well up in her eyes. "My son died two months ago."

This struck close to home with me, the safety of my sons somewhat being a catalyst for this resolution. So I break my policy about public praying. Right there, in the middle of that rest stop, I wrap my arms around her and whisper a prayer for her broken heart. One mother to another. I couldn't tell you now what those words were. It doesn't matter.

The woman called her husband over to meet me, then we spoke awhile about my trip but I wasn't thinking anymore about making great time to get to my destination.

Today, the journey really was the purpose. The people that we meet along the way. But I hope that prayer is lingering somehow even as I write this story. I hope that prayers are timeless and everlasting. I'm hoping that even now those words can be deeply felt and that her heart is continuing to heal.

THE ORPHAN

Every child you encounter is a divine appointment.

—WESS STAFFORD

THERE'S A BABY CRYING. I CAN HEAR IT FROM UPSTAIRS, locked away in my room at a bed-and-breakfast. I'm here to hide and to write, but my mother ears keep picking up the baby's cry. It sounds pretty new.

I go back to my books, pen, and paper, and try to focus on my work, but a little while later the baby is still crying. I feel sorry for the tired parents and the poor baby, who is sick maybe or just overly tired. The baby keeps crying and I put down my journal and move toward the door. I hate to interfere but can't someone hear the baby? Did they go out and leave the baby?

I crack open the door and the cries grow louder. I stand a moment, undecided, and then step out and pull my bedroom door closed behind me and quietly descend the staircase. The cries grow louder as I approach a bedroom on the first floor, the door is ajar and the room is dark. I call, "Hello? Is anyone there?" And then I push the door gently until it opens into darkness, a large empty bed, a tiny crib, and in the crib something moving, something now that sounds scared and desperate and angry. "Anyone here?" I call again for the entire house to hear, but there is no response so I wander in and look into the crib. A small baby, the blanket has fallen down over its face, the feet squirming and kicking and it's screaming muffled screams. I pull back the blanket, uncover its face, and lift the baby to my chest, cuddling it and saying "There, there," the way a mama does. I pace the floor a bit, walk into the living room, and the baby quiets, looks at me with watery blue eyes. The hair is dark and sweaty. I find a rocker and place the baby on my shoulder, patting and rocking, wondering where the parents are and who this precious bit belongs to.

I'm not thinking of my sons, not drawing from any huge mother instinct. I'm just thinking, *Whose baby is this? Why do I have the baby? I'm supposed to be writing and resting. Now, I'm stuck with a strange baby. I may be stuck with this baby all night. Maybe forever. There, there now, baby. It will be all right. Why, just look at all that hair you have.*

The baby quits crying, and she gets really quiet and relaxed in that baby weight kind of way. She kinda sighs and snuggles against my chest. Now, I'm just rocking the baby. We develop a rhythm and I no longer care about someone coming to claim her, to relieve me of my burden. Here is this tiny, little soul, about to be thrust out into the messy human world, and no matter what, she will need all the prayer she can get, just like the rest of us. Then before I think about it, I'm praying with all my might for this baby, quietly from the center of my soul. It's a girl, I see, new-born, almost brand-new, with little pierced ears. I pray for her future and her safekeeping, for her purpose and destiny in God.

Eventually, a woman comes downstairs and says, "Oh my! The baby woke? I'm so sorry." But I'm not sorry and the sleeping baby on my shoulder no longer seems sorry either. The baby seems beautiful and content as I pass her into wait-ing arms. "My granddaughter's baby," she explains. "She's young, having problems. I don't think they can keep her." The baby's eyes catch her expression like a question mark. "I'm too old for an infant so she'll have to go to a home." She looks at the little face, catches a glimpse of what might have been. "It's such a shame."

Then I wonder about happenstance, of strange babies crying in the dark, of strangers praying for destinies to unfold the way they should. A baby falls into my hands late at night while on retreat? One with an unclear future being cast out onto a long road of maybes. I don't think it was chance at all. Any more than my resolution to pray was just a quick, and easy, idea.

THE SHAPE OF PRAYER

Most men pray for power, the strength to do things.
Few people pray for love, the quality to be someone.

—ROBERT FOSTER

PRAYER TAKES ON DIFFERENT FORMS. I'M THINKING IT COULD be an offer of a ride on a rainy afternoon to an old woman walking down the road. Or a cup of coffee and a meal to someone standing outside a restaurant with nothing but time. Sometimes it's just not standing by and doing nothing.

I hear the young girl in front of me lean in and whisper to the server, "How much for just a vegetable?"

He offers up the price and I hear her say, "For one? Just one?" He nods and then she steps out of line, turns to go, her head hung down.

"Hold on," I say, then step out of line and raise my arm as if I'm hailing a cab. "Just hold up," I call to her in a very non-dignified way. She turns around, her hand to her face, where

she is wiping away tears. "Come here," I say, and motion her
to hurry up, trying to use my kindest hurry motion. As she
approaches, I tell her, "I've got this one. Just order lunch."

"No, no, it's okay."

"Really. Allow me. I've got this."

"Are you sure?" She's a tiny thing wearing camouflage
pants and a T-shirt that could swallow her.

"Oh yeah, I'm sure. Only deal is you have to get everything." "Everything" means the lunch special. It's a Tennessee package deal: a meat and three vegetables, cornbread,
and iced tea. The works.

Sometimes the end of the rope is so near the surface of a
person's soul. And we never know, never, ever, ever know
how one more drop of rain might just push that person
over the edge into the abyss. Or how one word from us, one
small offering, one lunch, one prayer, might be the difference that pulls them back from the brink.

"What's your name?"

"Jewel," she says and looks down at her plate. "Thank
you so much. You have no idea how much this means. You
just don't know."

"I've been there, Jewel. You just have a better day."

I *have* been there. The fact is, I do so know how one
stranger can help another survive this thing called life.
Then I leave her to her food. I don't suggest we eat together
because I don't want her thinking she has to eat with gratitude. "Take care," I tell her, wishing her a rich life. A little

silent prayer for her success in life. For the rough spots to be made smooth.

One tiny word. How can it matter so much? But it does. Time and time again. Our connection to one another, our need for one another, is reaffirmed over and over again.

I was at one of my favorite delis ordering a few Italian hoagies. Just another day for me. But when that man stepped up to take my order, it was time to make more than an ordinary kind of exchange. See, I'd been watching him as I priced the cheese, checked out this week's specials.

He reveals that his name is Ronnie when I tell him that today I'm after more than just my order, I'm looking for a stranger. I can still hear his response ringing in my ears. I've had people cry on me, hug me, and thank me silently, deeply with their eyes, but this man is the only person who has ever acted as though he just won the lottery. Really. You would have thought after I'd shared my resolution, told him that today he was my person, that I'd said, "And now, step right up because you, sir, have won a million dollars!"

"And today it's me?! Today I'm the stranger? I'm the one?!"

Here's the thing: He's friendly to start with. A man full of smiles, light on his toes like a boxer in the ring. There's a quickness about him. I'm always looking to my right and left before I tell anyone anything. I'm always trying to keep things quiet, not cause a scene or a stir. But this time a scene may be inevitable because this guy is so loud and animated.

"Me?" He takes three full steps back. "And you picked me." Now, he steps forward again. "Man, you have *no idea* how much I needed that."

"That so?"

"Oh, especially today. You have no idea what's going on. Man! Imagine that today it's me!" He raises his voice in absolute, unabashed delight.

I don't think I've ever won anything. I've tried. I've entered a few contests here and there, one for a trip to Italy I was sure that I had nailed, but I never received the call. And every other thing I've "won" has come with a special price. Oh, that free trip? Well, surprise, there's six hundred dollars in airfare fees tied to that free trip. Or there's a three-hour pitch for a thingamajig that I have to sign up for to be a lifetime member in exchange for my free television. But today I get to be the person with the prize to give. Only in this case, there isn't any money at all. No sweepstakes check. Just the offering of prayer, the promise of a prayer. From the smile on Ronnie's face, that was enough.

Occasionally, I see Ronnie after this but he really doesn't place me. Like when you see someone and try to remember them, where you know them from, but you can't actually put the memories together in such a way that the face falls into place. But that's not the case with Jewel. By chance I see her again.

Months later, I'm walking down the hall of a local college and there she is—there is Jewel, but she has a different air, as if light travels with her. That day in the line looks like a distant, murky past.

I almost passed her—there was such a visible difference in her that she was almost unrecognizable. "Hey! How are you doing?"

"Oh, hey there." She's all smiles. "It's really good. School's going great. My grades are good and I'm about to graduate." And then she is going on about something about her classes and art something or other, but I am honestly not listening to the details. I'm looking at the difference in her face. At how very much alive she is.

If I contributed in any small way to the change of events in her life, if that one day helped just get her through a stormy, hungry afternoon, then I have to remind myself that the simplest acts, the tiniest things, in a rather ordinary day can have an impact that is larger than my understanding and that I must not stop. I must remain connected.

PRAYERS FOR THE CHILDREN

Wishing will never be a substitute for prayer.

—ED COLE

M Y COUSIN E-MAILS ME FROM A CLINIC SHE WORKS AT IN Georgia that the H1N1 virus has invaded. The worst hit, she says, are the children and the clinic is full of them. Many have had to be taken from the clinic to a hospital by ambulance. She asks me to pray for them. Tells me that they are all so sick and so sad.

I write back that certainly I will pray for the children. Then I offer up one of my shoeshine prayers. Polished and quick as lightning. God, help the children and make them well. Amen. Job done. Check that box.

Except I woke up this morning thinking of those children again. My grandchildren are seven and three, my niece and nephew eight and five. The news of this outbreak brings me new concern that suddenly the outbreak will continue to spread, have dire consequences, that my children, the ones in my life and closest to my heart, will be affected. My concern for them is greater than my best prayers for those sick clinic children. The window of my soul is obviously a little clouded.

The children in the clinic don't have a tangible, vested place in my life. I don't have their *stories*, the funny little things they've said, and the way they first learned to walk or talk. I've never seen them in the fullness of their lives and three-dimensionally. They have become statistics, numbers, flashed images on the evening news. Victims of some distant outbreak, famine, flood, or catastrophic event. I can shake my head in sadness and offer up my quick and easy prayers. Normally.

But this morning those children in that clinic are my strangers. Not just one of them, but a collective. I make a purpose to really pray. To be willing to hit the pause button on my agenda, to delay breakfast for a little while so that I can actually, really offer up a prayer. So I do that. I pray for the sick, for the people taking care of them around the clock, for the worried parents watching over them. I pray all the mighty prayers I can think of to get the job done.

And maybe what matters most is that suddenly I care. I really care about these particular sick children in a Georgia clinic that I've never seen. And it's that caring, that compassion, that might just make a difference. I carry them with me through the day, and the thought of them is in my heart as I go to sleep.

Then a thought occurs to me and I wonder, Could the stranger any of us pray for be more than just one person? Could it be a neighborhood or city? A refugee camp or a state? The truth is I have no barometer, no fast and furious rule book on this thing. Just a leading and a resolution. I don't know what I'm doing at all. Except for this—this praying thing. I continue doing this day after day. And I keep changing. From the inside out.

BLESS THE CHILD

More things are wrought by prayer
than this world dreams of.

—ALFRED, LORD TENNYSON

I'M IN A COFFEE SHOP PICKING UP A FAST LATTE. NORMALLY, I'm a drive-through woman. But today I'm searching through their selection of CDs while I'm waiting. I love to find new music to feature on my radio program. While I'm waiting, I notice a young woman watching me rather seriously. She smiles awkwardly when I see her, hiding her face quickly back in the book before her. I wait for the latte, consider my options, and check my watch. It's there again, that familiar pull and, along with it, the question that has become practically my constant companion.

Finally, I take the latte, the new CD, and approach her. I kneel down on one knee next to her, trying to speak quietly. I don't want the other patrons listening in on our conversation. This close I can see that she is young, much younger than I first thought. Schoolgirl young. I don't want to frighten her, but I'm already this close. I explain my purpose to her, tell her she stood out to me as someone special, and I just wanted her to know. I hover nearby for a minute even after she whispers, "Thank you."

"Need a prayer for anything special?"

The stereo is playing Sheryl Crow's new song. I listen to the words while I wait. It's a gift sometimes, this ability to wait. The girl is nervous and I can see it. Not like first day of school jitters, but the kind of nervous that comes from watching shadows in the corner. I can feel that kind of nervous. It spreads, makes the hairs on the back of your arm rise.

She nods *yes* without hesitation. "My mom."

I wait, as she seems to try to put the words together, wondering if I should prod, ask her anything more, but then it isn't necessary. She offers up the words, still whispering, hesitant as if the coffee shop walls have extra eyes.

"My mom," she says again, "she's bipolar and . . ." Her words trip, stumble, and retreat back in on themselves. I tell her I'll pray for her mom. Then I add, "But you should know, I'll be praying for you, too."

At her age, I could have used a stranger's prayer on any given day. But this girl doesn't just have the regular teenage challenges to face. Home is supposed to be a safe place, but one day she may walk through the door and find that things have changed during the day while she was away. I have

friends and family members diagnosed as bipolar. Sometimes they take their medicine and sometimes they don't.
There are seasons in their lives that are relatively peaceful
and seasons without a blink of sleep or peace.

My heart bends a little as I pray for her and I imagine her
keeping elements of her home life private, or when I think
about her needing to be an adult before her time. To try to
fix things, to keep things quiet and running smoothly.

No wonder she looked so much older at first glance. She is.

Strange Signs and Smoking Trucks

The less you know, the more you believe.

—BONO

I'M RIDING IN THE FRONT SEAT OF A TOW TRUCK. OH, DON'T ask. Seriously. This isn't my day to discuss the particulars of why or how I got here. Just that I had a little problem with my vehicle that was supposed to be fixed by now but it isn't. So I'm now riding in a tow truck. A smoking tow truck. I think it's a 1968 model. The driver is sweating and the gears grinding and my to-do list of errand running is out the window.

My day started out simply enough. I was in my little dream vehicle—the one that replaced my long-lasting, dependable Nissan that finally bit the dust—but in the middle of a day planned with more than could possibly fit within it, my car rattles and rolls, shakes at an intersection, and dies, as the engine light begins flashing.

I just had this problem fixed. There should be nothing wrong with this baby. This is my very first day back in the car after it came out of the shop. After days of being grounded, my list of things I wanted to accomplish is about to topple me. I have last minute birthday presents to shop for, mailings, a veritable catchall list of catch-ups.

But then the shimmy and the shake at the red light. Me being stalled on the side of the road and making rude phone calls. Long gone are my altruistic enlightened moments when I pray for goodness for every soul I come in contact with. I'm just teary and tired. The driver has had to try a few times to get my car loaded on his truck. He looks more than a tad worried as he tries to shift again and keeps his eye on the rearview mirror. He's wondering if he's going to lose that vehicle back there. I just know he is. So am I.

I don't want to have car trouble right now. I don't want to be angry with the insurance company or the mechanic that they recommended. I just want a vehicle that is running properly in a town where getting around without one isn't much of an option. I drive through a lot of woods and trees to get home. The buses don't exactly run by my house, there are no subways, and trains are for freight and only heard in the distance. Personal transportation is a requirement.

So I'm sitting in this smoking, belching truck, we're caught in traffic at a bad time of day, and now the driver isn't just worried about the gears grinding and losing the vehicle, he's also very concerned about the truck overheating. I'm beginning to think we may need another tow truck to get us both out of here. It's going from inconvenient and expensive to worse.

But then I spot a man standing by the side of road. One might assume he is homeless. Or at least out of work. Well, the sign he's holding—the one that says, OUT OF WORK— might be a giveaway. I think the sign also says something about needing help or something, but I'm not really reading it. I need help, too. But then he does the oddest thing. He looks at me—and with that one look, he takes in the steaming, smoking tow truck pulling the car, me in the front seat, the expression on my face, and the driver's expression— and then he smiles softly and lifts two fingers in what has become a universal symbol of peace.

Peace.

I get it. Peace in the midst of the turmoils and troubles of life. That weird abiding peace that helps us reach our destinations in life. Whether they be spiritual quests involving mountaintops or literally trying to make it to the next gas station, the element of peace, that perfect possession of the peace of our souls, seems to help with the journey more than anything. It's easier to pray for a stranger when we possess that place where we can walk on the waters that trouble us most, the tides of our emotions rising and rolling inside.

I smile back at him and lift my hand, two fingers raised.

Peace, brother. Saying prayers for you.

I'd like to say that I traveled the rest of the road so turned around that the driver and I sang "Me and Bobby McGee" the rest of the way. But that's not how it happened. He continued to worry about the traffic and overheating. I tried to stay below the boiling point of angry. I did take a few deep breaths and make small talk with the driver about his grandson, who kept calling him on the cell phone. He wanted his pawpaw to come pick him up to go look at a go-cart for sale. What I really love is the fact that the driver answered the phone in spite of the truck smoldering, him trying to pull me and the jeep up the hill.

The man by the side of the road, his expression, and his message—well, those aren't the kinds of things that are really only for that moment. Good messages are eternal. There's no end to them in the long run. I could pull out that man's message to me on any given day, open it, and receive it. And turn around and give it away. And every time I do, I'll say a prayer for him.

PERSPECTIVE AND PERCEPTION

You can safely assume you've created God
in your own image when it turns out that
God hates all the same people you do.

—ANNE LAMOTT

THERE'S AN OLD CARTOON I REMEMBER OF SEVEN BLIND
men describing an elephant. Each one happens to
be touching a specific part of the elephant's anatomy and
thereby perceives that the entire elephant can be described
from that myopic point of view. It seems to me in many
ways in our culture or society we are encouraged to look
at things just that way. Judge the whole by the one. Lump
people into huge disparaging categories at a glance. One
thing is for certain in this life, we are taught early to choose
sides. We can say we don't, but we do. We can even try not
to, but the habit clings to us from bygone days. It's one of

the first things we learned in grade school. There are sides to
be decided, names to be called out. You must play for team
A or team B. The green team or the blue team. You must
associate yourself with the one side of the playing field.
That example is followed by all the school activities consist-
ing of us against them, one school against the one across
town, one city against another, and on to state and finally,
hopefully, nationals. I'm not against teams or the great fun
of sportsmanship. I have a few blue ribbons stashed somewhere for schoolyard soccer, and I love the Olympic Games.
What I'm against is the concept of "the other." Not that it's
not normal for us to align ourselves with those of like mind
and passions, but I'm troubled when "the other" becomes
someone we've unjustly named the enemy. Like our dry
cleaner who has Republican stickers in his window, or the
diner owner who declares openly he's a Democrat.

Unfortunately our choices become prejudices that can
keep us from playing nice with each other. And while my
personal prejudices don't involve color, creed, or religion,
trust me, I still have a few. But I'm working on them.

One of the things that I discovered during this resolution is that I pray for people no matter what side of the
fence they're on politically, spiritually, culturally, or eco-
nomically. I pray for them without knowing their histories,
their zip codes, or how they voted in the most recent elec-
tion. All right. Sometimes. I have talked to people with yard
signs different than my own might be if I had one, bumper

stickers that were different from mine if I had one. I'm very much interested in exploring the ties that bind us, not the ones that divide us. Still, my opinions sometimes ride high in my back pocket, visible from a distance.

On a few days during this year I prayed for people who are famous in the political arena. Personally, I don't think I agree with their political views and policies and I don't know that I like either one of them so much, but then I don't really know them. I just know their processed images, their sound bites, their faces flashed and frozen throughout time on pages of magazines and newspapers.

Here's the surprising part to me. The prayers for these politicians (both Democrat and Republican, for the record), for people of every faith and background, were sincere. Heartfelt. And my amazing discovery is that the longer you pray for someone, the more you lose that crust of ambivalence, that twinge of not liking them. Those things fall away, and instead sometimes there's just a flash of comprehension, compassion, and care so that if that person walked through the door, I'd be pleased to meet them in that moment.

Somewhere in that slice of time I spent praying, wishing, hoping for good things in their lives, for the crooked places to be made straight, for their enemies to be at peace with them, I became less frustrated by their presence.

Today I prayed for someone different than I am. I don't know exactly how different. For all I know, we both love the same authors and perfume, but her appearance is different.

She wears a burka. I'm a little more into blue jeans. A burka is the kind of thing that seems so otherworldly in America. It reminds some of us that there is a country that gave birth to this type of dress for women. Unfortunately, some of the people from that country, associated with that country, have declared themselves the enemies of my people, my country. But the dress itself, the headdress, the woman wearing it and walking past me in the rain, she is not my enemy. Today she is my stranger.

I've actually been having a bad day. The kind where you have a flat tire on the way to work, and then you find out you've overdrawn your checking account and the paycheck you were expecting is being held up for some red tape reason for two more weeks. Lovely kinds of days where the drivel of daily life could drive you insane in the middle of an ocean full of blessings. It's just the kind of day where the drivel is a continual drop, drop, drop. Soon quite literally it begins to drizzle, a steady cold, chilly rain. How poetically perfect.

Then I see the girl with the burka moving in between the rain. I reach out and lightly touch her arm as she passes me. "Excuse me? Do you mind if I ask your name?"

"Faith," she says, eyes smiling, aglow in the circle of that black.

Of course it is. On a pop-quiz, the-dog-ate-my-homework kind of a day, of course, of all people I stop on this drizzling day, it's someone named Faith. In a burka no less.

"Faith, I do so love your name. Now, here's the thing.

Prayers and blessings said. Good life and true love and happiness abounding." This is not exactly what I told her, but it was close to it. She smiled again, shivered, and thanked me.

I watched her walk away for just a minute, disappearing across the campus. What I wanted to say was, "No—thank *you*, Faith. For your name and for your smile."

Perhaps someday in a perfect world we will not judge each other by our differences but manage to celebrate them instead. Maybe that perfect world will include a few inherent rules such as respect for differences of creed and color, race and religion, politics and neighborhoods, cat people and dog people. Maybe we can recognize these things without allowing them to determine who we are or who we're not allowed to be.

For me, taking these incredible chances every day to speak to people, to pray for people I don't love, don't even like, or who are from a different ideological or political background, has brought me closer to a state of personal grace where loving them is possible. Even probable.

But life is a messy affair, full of opinions and motives, emotions and histories, friendships and enemies. Perhaps it is our human nature to form allegiances. And it's one of the very reasons that I love this prayer resolution so much—I just keep praying no matter what our differences may be. Even if you get your news from Fox and I get mine from the BBC, if you attend a different church or no church at all, if you like strawberries and they make me break out in hives, it makes no difference because in the big scheme of things, it really doesn't matter.

But here's what does.

On some days I pray for more than one person. Because I can. Because I want to. Because my heart has been softened by this year of connecting with the world around me. Just the other day I passed a man on his riding lawn mower wearing a white hat. He smiled and waved and I waved back, and in that moment, special stranger of the day status or not, it was my automatic response to wish blessings on his life and say a quick prayer for his health and happiness. And the rest of my day continued that way. A cashier, the woman at the insurance company, the librarian—I prayed for them all.

Then I began to wonder: Could it be possible for us to move through our day on a wave of prayer, receiving and giving, offering silent words, thoughts, good intent to the people that we meet along the way? Could our cities have undercurrents of prayer that course through the business of our lives? Would there be a tangible feeling, a current that pulls at us, whispering for us to remember we are part of a larger, vast ocean teeming with life and stories? If I can begin to live this way for a moment, for part of a day, for a week at a time, then yes, I can imagine a place where people find a common ground of timelessness and understanding and goodwill. And I like that.

Missed Chances

Prayer is a triumph, in whatever form.

—TERRI GUILLEMETS

S HE HAUNTS ME, SHE DOES. ALL NIGHT LONG AND INTO THIS morning. It's a rather silly thing that someone in passing could make me feel this way, but missed opportunities have perhaps become as much a part of my life as praying for strangers. It isn't that I don't pray—I do. It's that the opportunity for that human connection is lost and maybe it was meant to happen for a reason. Not only meant to happen but potentially on any given day I bump into someone and feel a special connection.

Yesterday, it was a woman in a grocery store. An older woman who had left her shopping cart, walked back to pick up a can of tomatoes, and when she did, our eyes met. Immediately I said, "And how are you today?"

She reminded me of my grandmother. Her eyes, her mannerisms. And she was delighted to have someone ask.

She responded just as quick as you please with her own version of, "Good and you?"

Then I kept walking as I said, "Fine, fine."

I don't know why I didn't stop and tell her—*Tonight before I fall asleep, I'm going to say a special blessing for you. Maybe two.* I wish I had found out her name, gotten a part of her story. I'm so frustrated by this experience today, this unfinished, undone business of being personal, that it makes me want to become . . . well, I started to say a crazy person. Maybe, what I mean is an *extrovert*. And with that thought I had to just drop everything and go look up the word *extrovert* in one of my favorite dictionaries—*The Reader's Digest Great Encyclopedic Dictionary*. It explains to me that "extroversion" is "the turning of one's self-interest toward objects and actions outside the self rather than toward one's own thoughts or feelings." Funny, that's not what I have in mind when I think of an extrovert. I generally think of someone who talks rather much and does so in a loud voice.

I think—and this is a confession of the most brutal kind—that I have believed introverts to be superior in some ways to extroverted people. My extroverted friends, I beg your apologies. It's not that I feel myself superior to any number of outgoing and dynamite friends with a Gregorian, nonshy nature. It's that I value silence to a high degree. A very high degree. I think of monastic orders such as the cloistered nuns or the desert monks.

I don't mind spending the day, or days, alone and in

silence. The longer the alone, the easier the silence becomes because the spirit finds its centered, quiet place. Oh, trust me, my mind and body reel at first. I have a hundred friends and family members whom I want to call to say, *I'm here in this silent place and so now I'm going to go be silent but first—what's up with you and all your children, grandchildren, work, play, and seen any good movies lately?* But eventually, I'll wrestle my habit of business into a type of holy silence where I can hear myself think clearly. I value this so much I encourage other friends to do the same. *Oh, c'mon,* I say, *just three days and nights of no cells, no e-mail, and no television—not even a great book to distract you. Just you and, ummm, say a journal or two and a friend and absolute quiet for seventy-two hours.*

"I would die," my cousin tells me. And while this isn't true, I know that she believes it to be so.

Other friends tell me that they would just go crazy. Really, really crazy.

My big question is, Why? What is it about our society that has made us so dependent on noise and distraction? And if even the most extroverted of us are so dependent in general, so used to the noise, the constant conversation, why is it so difficult to tell one soul a day, three times a week, or once a month—that we are wishing them goodness and peace and mercy?

I think I must discover a greater balance in my life. I believe that this prayer resolution is leading the way, showing me the way to do that. I believe that it is leading me down

a path that I never intended to take. I do believe I must keep
my silent moments a part of my life always, where I carve out
time for the quiet my soul requires to heal and create. But
I'm thinking that the time that I'm not away, in my space,
in my room, in my car, walking through my trees, should
be involved with other people. Not just the ones that I have
chosen deliberately but the ones that through circumstance
have chosen me. I'm thinking that I can introduce myself to
the woman in the grocery store, ask her maybe more than
how she's doing as I walk past almost quick enough to not
even hear the answer. She wanted more from that moment,
more of a connection. The funny, incredible thing is that in
the end, I did, too.

I miss my grandmother. I miss the age of her. The way she
just knew things that younger people don't know. Younger
being all ages before her. She's been gone from here for a
long, long time now, and yet I miss the comfort of her presence. Sometimes, on good nights, I'll dream we had a visit.
But those nights are few and far between. Years and years
will pass but then there will be that morning when I wake
and it's as if I was sitting in her kitchen visiting. I wake up
feeling fully, unconditionally loved.

But here was this woman, my grandmother's age the last
time I saw her, wanting to speak just a little longer. Perhaps
she was a gift to me in the odd ways that a person can be. A
newfound friend or a someone who steps out of nowhere
to help. Perhaps she could have filled in that gap my grand-

mother left just a little. Even if it was for one conversation. The two of us, I'm thinking, could have both used that. And maybe, I'll see her again. If not, perhaps someone like her who is maybe just this side of lonely and open for a new friend. And I promise I'll stop and visit a bit, and we'll both be better for it.

TIMING THE TALK

I greet you. Not quite as the world sends greetings,
but with profound esteem and with the prayer
that for you now and forever, the day breaks,
and the shadows flee away.

—FRA GIOVANNI GIOCONDO

I'M PLAYING IN THE MAKEUP SECTION OF THE DEPARTMENT store when I first see her. My cousin has brought me out with a list of things to accomplish. Being the very bad shopper person that I am, and she being the supreme shopper of all time, we have attempted to tackle this assignment together. Buy things for Mother, hit the makeup sale, and find earrings.

I'm playing with the lipsticks when I look up and see the woman talking to another cosmetic person a counter away. Just like that I think, *Oh, it's her.* One thing I love about this business with the strangers is when it happens that way, sneaking in the side door of my life. When I'm considering meat in the grocery store or trying to figure out exactly what is in fruit juice that the label says "contains 10 percent juice." What exactly is the other 90 percent? And then I look up and see an old man standing next to me trying his best to read the juice label, too, and I think, *Snap—it's him.* But today, instead of juice, I'm studying fuchsias and reds and browns and the latest neutrals. I can't interrupt my stranger while she's talking, I'll just wait on her and catch her when she's through. Just say a few words.

Then I wander over to the mascaras and the eye shadows and start playing with the testers like I am five years old. There are seven different shades of brown, three greens, two blues, one smoky gray on the back of my hand. I look up and the woman's gone. It could have been five minutes or twenty-five. I can be oblivious to the hands of time.

I look toward the other side of the counter, search the area around cosmetics and perfumes. Gone. A familiar sense of loss falls upon me. I get it every time I should have told someone and didn't for whatever reason—too rushed, too lazy, too distracted. Or in this case, with all good intentions to speak but to no avail. It always leaves emptiness in me or a sense of missed opportunity. Similar to the time I passed Bill Murray in a restaurant and meant to tell him, "Personally, I loved *The Razor's Edge*, and because you made that movie, I read everything Somerset Maugham ever wrote. I just thought you should know that." But being out of my element, maybe a tad shy, or even starstruck, I never said a word and that fact has haunted me. The feeling is just like that. When I'm meant to tell, when a person comes into focus in my life in a special way, the not telling is haunting. It follows me much more than any hurried or lukewarm response I could ever get, because while telling risks personal rejection, not telling creates what-ifs and might-have-beens. Those trouble me for some time.

Then just as I'm searching for my cousin, the woman emerges from the purse department. It's a wonder that I didn't tackle her, I was so determined in my enthusiasm to not let her get away from me a second time.

"May I ask your name?"

And that's how the conversation with this beautiful person begins. It emerges into something else, and my guess is that fifteen minutes later we're still speaking. Talking about the fact that her husband passed away a few years ago, that she volunteers at the local hospital, and how much my stopping her means to her. She wants to know my name, and more about how the year's been going.

I tell her that the stories are being written now, that they'll be in a book someday.

"Oh, I want to read that book. I'm going to get it if I'm still around when it comes out."

There have been a few things weighing heavy on Virginia. Her health—really a multitude of new health problems—is one of the things. But just telling her that she's my stranger seems to lighten that load visibly. We hug each other before we go and I tell her she'll be around for some time to come. Because I believe it to be so.

My cousin's been playing at another makeup counter waiting on me.

"Where do you know her from?"

"Who?"

"The woman you've been talking to back there."

"Never met her before just now. She's my stranger."

"You're kidding me, right?"

"Nope. Not kidding. Just met her. She's a widow, lost her husband, volunteers at the hospital. Very nice lady."

"That's amazing. From the way you were talking, I thought you knew her well."

I know her now. At least better than before never speaking. It's an odd thing, it is, this prayer business.

"I almost missed her," I say. We step out into what's left of the day. I put on my sunglasses and start the car with my cousin still whispering, "Amazing," and me thinking of the tiny threads of happenstance that connect one life to another. How fragile and unpredictable they are and the unexpected joys in connecting with a life we never would have known.

PRAYERS OF THE PEOPLE

Prayer gives a man the opportunity of getting
to know a gentleman he hardly ever meets.
I do not mean his maker, but himself.

—WILLIAM INGE

O N MY LAST VISIT TO NEW YORK, I HAD THE PLEASURE OF
visiting Saint Patrick's Cathedral. I arrived and walked
up those huge steps and, once inside, discovered it's not
the hushed, quiet atmosphere of a deserted cathedral on a
downtown afternoon like the historic Episcopal Cathedral
on Broadway in Nashville. It's part tourist stop. There are
guards checking backpacks, there are people taking pictures
everywhere. There are people taking pamphlets. And yet, there
is, in the midst of the bodies, of the bustle/hustle, at least an
attempted hush. The way people walk into a space and visibly
try to observe the difference, the shift from one energy into
another. The way a person with really squeaky shoes walks
on their tiptoes to no avail.

Now, for those of you who are not Cathedral junkies and don't visit monasteries or trippy holy places when you are on vacation, I'll describe a few things for you. From the back of Saint Patrick's you have the bodies and backpacks. Lots. Then there is a table and security-guard-people types because now everywhere you go (and I mean everywhere) apparently backpacks are suspect and must be searched. Then there are three aisles. The right, left, and middle. And on the right and left aisles there are small places to pray. Each of these depicts a different scene, each with candles for prayer purposes, many of which have been lit by people recently stopping to pray or by tourists who think lighting a candle is the ritual connected to taking a picture. People who don't normally light a candle, but do it anyway thinking they're doing it out of respect.

As you draw deeper into the center of the cathedral, you begin to notice that the quiet expands. There is a balloon of silence. Once you begin to let your restless mind actually rest, you notice that some people are kneeling, lifting up shifting words to the unseen in earnest. People walk more softly here, pocket those cameras by instinct even before they see the sign that says NO PHOTOS AND NO TALKING BEYOND THIS POINT. And there, beyond the front of the cathedral, beyond the altar at the front of the church, lies another chapel, hidden by its distance and by its placement into the deepest parts of the deep of the cathedral.

All is white. The light, the marble. I slide into a pew, sit small and tired and silent. And wait. Not for anything. Not a sign or an answer—just waiting. Maybe for the otherworldliness to take over from the busy bustle of Fifth Avenue, for the other to seep all the way in, beneath my skin, into my veins, the marrow of my bones. And then what I notice more than anything else is the unorganized whisper of a prayer here and a prayer there. Softly, like newborn feathers, voices that are really too low to be heard at all. Perhaps I felt them first. They were in different languages, English, Spanish, an Oriental tongue I could not distinguish. All melting pot music. And what I loved in that moment was that the truck-driving blue-collar guy was on equal ground with the lady born to live and die with money. A young girl, an old man, two matching sisters kneeling like bookends and then helping one another to their feet, all in the deepest, quietest part of Saint Patrick's on a Thursday afternoon on Fifth Avenue in Manhattan. These people who had come for something other than a picture or a postcard. They had purposed themselves into the deepest of the deep, not stopping at some tiny prayer corner, not just stopping at some symbolic turn of design, but finding their way into what might be the holy of holies.

Then I thought of how this widely blessed and beautiful collection of faces were all, at that moment, on common ground. No matter what their state, their place, their occupation, or their address—Park Avenue or a park bench—they were equals before God. And those whispers rolled up and out before the flickering lights, making their way far beyond that marble ceiling.

And all I could do was whisper, *Amen* and *Amen* and *Amen*.

BLESSINGS

You must pray that the way be long,
full of adventures and experiences.

—CONSTANTINE PETER CAVAFY

I'VE PRAYED FOR PEOPLE AT THIS PLACE BEFORE. UTILITY COMpanies seem to stir up those waters. I've plucked strangers from the line in the water department, from over the phone with the electric company, talking to customer service people for the telephone, and whispered about a prayer behind the glass to the cashiers taking payments everywhere.

For the record, I'm the kind of person who could be typing these words as the power is turned off and the lights fade out around me, and the faucet drips dry. I have always related to the woman in *Romancing the Stone* who is writing, writing, writing, and finishing a novel as the trash piles up around her and the cat runs out of food. Maybe because of this, oftentimes I'm having to take my check downtown to the company because I forgot to put it in the mail before the due date.

Today is one of the days that I have decided I just will not tell a stranger anything at all about this praying business. I plan on keeping everything to myself, silently holding on to the images of faces and saying prayers over them before I go to sleep. Usually, when I make up my mind about that, when I am most serious in my determination, I end up telling the next person I see. That is just about the case today as a woman moves ahead of me in the line. When I see her, I know I have to speak to her. I just have to.

I get through the customer service line as fast as I can and rush to the door. She is wearing a big black jacket and sensible shoes. There she is slowly making her way across the parking lot. I go after her.

"Excuse me, excuse me, but what is your name if you don't mind me asking?"

"Kate," she says.

"What a lovely name. I have a character in a book I wrote named Kate. It's an old family name, too. My aunt's name was Kate."

"Really? And you're a writer."

"Yes, ma'am, I am, but I stopped you for another reason. I've been doing this thing now for a year."

"What's that?" Thankfully, I can see she's in no hurry.

"Praying for people. That's what I've been doing. Just a different stranger I see every day and today you're my stranger."

"Well, God bless you! I sure do need it."

"How so? What do you need prayer for?"

"Mostly my health, you know? Just trying to get around."
She moves back and forth some on her feet. They look like
they'd prefer to be propped up right now.

"Yes, ma'am. I understand. I'll be praying for you, for
everything. For good health and all good things."

"Well, let me just give you a hug before you go," Kate says.
And she leans over and wraps me, smothers me in those big
arms. Oh, I'll take that hug and a million like them from all
the Kates of the world. I'll take these momentary blessed
moments of human relating. While I'm saying a prayer
for Kate and her health, I'm going to offer up a prayer of
thanksgiving at the same time. Just a quick one that says to
the Creator—thanks for making the Kates of the world. For
all the hugs that they've been passing out for generations of
generations. The world needs more of them.

THE DELIGHT OF
SANDY LEE

Love one another.

—JESUS

THERE ARE TIMES THAT PRAYING FOR A STRANGER, OR AT least talking to a stranger, comes easier than others. I suspect it's probably easier to talk to strangers in the South. Personally, I think it's because there is so much space out in the more rural areas and because of this, a quick conversation standing in a checkout line doesn't encroach on our private bubbles. I say that, but when visiting the city, I talk to strangers there, too. Just not when we're all walking down the sidewalk at that lightning pace. I once remarked to my writer friend Alex Strauss that we could sort of meander our way down the street to the theater. She said, "We don't do that here."

"Why?"

"I don't know, but we don't. We never have."

"But, Alex, we have plenty of time. We're not in a hurry."

"We are," she tells me. "We're in a hurry to get there. Then we can wait."

That's my friend and I can't imagine her living anywhere else in the world other than Manhattan. I love her energy and the electric volt that is New York. And I love the strangers who are not meandering down the sidewalks. Life just moves at a faster pace. You can feel it the moment you arrive, walk the streets, or just sit and watch everyone else doing the same.

Today, I'm a long way from New York. I'm standing in the backwoods of Tennessee at a deli counter waiting my turn in line except our line is more of a horizontal agreement. A kind of *No, it's okay—really—you go first* affair.

While it may be a little more relaxed when it comes to talking to strangers in the South, I'm still thinking—*I'm not telling today*. Then I turn to the woman to my left with a simple, "How're you doing?"

This is a new thing for me. I used to try to tell people as quick as I could—*Today you're my stranger, I'm praying for you, have a great day*. But now, I'm beginning to go a little slower, realizing I won't self-destruct when I drop the word *prayer* and neither will the other person. We either have a few moments or we don't, and unless we are rushing to catch a red-eye out of town, we usually have more moments available for strangers than we realize.

"Are you doing all right?" I ask her.

"I'm hanging in there, but it sure is cold. It's hard on me."

Readers who live in places like Montana, Nebraska, Michigan, and New York might think cold in the Southern state of Tennessee to be a bit of a weak sentiment. But it's cold. She is right. We've had more snow than anyone can remember for years. More freezes. Tonight it's a blistering, windy cold.

"Hard on me, too. I'm from Florida. Don't handle the cold so well." I ask her name.

"Sandy Lee."

"Well, Sandy Lee, you better stay bundled up out there now."

"Isn't that the truth? Want to see what I got on?" She pulls up shirt number one to reveal the next one, and the next one, and then yet another one. Then she leans in and whispers, "You want to see what else I have on?" She looks over both shoulders and sees that for the moment the world is lost in itself, everyone focused on their own thing. "I got this a few months ago." She slides her shirt up to reveal a long, new scar running through her stomach and chest. "Heart surgery. Caught me by surprise. Today's the first day I been out of the house."

It's an angry pink line running straight up the center of her being. I think about what it's like to be cut open like that, to be so exposed to the world.

"Well, now isn't that something." Sometimes I slide into

my native tongue. It's what I call "back-road rural." This is one of those times. "Daddy had it done. It isn't easy but you can keep on going."

Then we talk about some other things that make me laugh now just thinking about them, but they are better left off the page.

Here's the thing about being Southern—some people might think Sandy Lee just a little too forward, sliding shirts up and showing a scar that size, but I'm here to tell you she is not. Down South you have to know when to look a stranger in the eye and decide whether or not to let them in on the sloppy, wonderful joke that is your life. Fortunately for me, Sandy Lee found me worthy of her story.

Somewhere in there I worked in that she was my stranger for the day because that's why I started the conversation with her in the first place. Then I told her to keep those layers on and walk careful on that icy ground.

Before I fell asleep, I lift up the character of the wild Sandy Lee, asking for all kinds of protections and life's beautiful satisfactions for my new friend. I sure hope I see her again.

Split Seconds and Passing Moments

If God can work through me,
he can work through anyone.

—SAINT FRANCIS OF ASSISI

I HAVE A LOT OF TIME INVESTED IN PEOPLE, SOME OF WHOM I've only met in a passing moment. I remember them just as well as the one who sat on the corner of a hotel parking lot and told me stories, or rode in my car for a few miles along the way, or the ones I now see on a regular basis in the course of my routines. There are now what seem like multitudes of people who were just a split second of eye contact, the brushing of hands, the whisper about a prayer, the collecting of their names into my pockets, their faces into my heart.

Here's the most important thing to me: These passing occurrences, these ever so brief moments with people, are just as illuminating and transformational. The connection just as real and everlasting. I've been whispering and passing people now for months.

Often it is the clerks, the customer service people, the cashier in the grocery stores, the man or woman behind the deli—these are my people on any given day and they just don't have the opportunity to stop and chat with me. Not that many of them wouldn't like to take a break, but they usually have eyes upon them, a line of people behind me waiting to order something, and many more hours of the clock ahead of them.

And in the midst of that reality, of all that going on in their lives, here this stranger steps up and says—*Hey, today you're my special stranger. I'll be thinking about you and saying special blessings for you today and before I go to sleep.* Only once in these situations have I received anything less than a breathless kind of *Oh, thank God.* It's in their eyes and more and more I can see why the eyes are described as the windows of the soul. The communication, the entire conversations I've had with people in these moments with their eyes, speak volumes. Words and words that there was no time and place to say, but it's as if they share their entire lives, their entire situations, with me in those brief passings. And while I have most of the names down right, it's that look in their eyes that I remember. *Thank you, thank you, thank you,* it speaks loudly time and again.

There's Peter at HG Hill. That young man in the deli

named Jason who had such a change come over him when I whispered those words to him that you would have sworn you saw the clouds part from over his head. When he said, "And you have a nice day now," he really meant it, from the bottom of his heart. He wasn't just talking from habit. There was the older woman in the produce department who, from the looks of her face lighting up, might as well have had an angel step down to tell her she'd been given a reprieve from death. Alicia, the young girl with braces working the cash register at a store in a rougher part of town and that silvered smile that just lit me up to pray for her future the best way I could. Just those few seconds and then I was in my car fervently praying for people to cross her path and help her fulfill her destiny. Barbara, who had such a beautiful smile and asked to give me a hug as she said, "Doesn't it just make you feel better to do this, too?" It does; she really got it. People in parking lots hurrying to their cars, the young, the aged, the in between. They are veritable snapshots that are part of my life now and I'm wondering where they all were before. Why was I not connecting on such a small, quick, but deep level previously? Was I somehow just that oblivious? Were they simply the sum of who my subconscious mind perceived them to be? The cashier, the server, the man on the phone, the stranger walking past me and therefore of no consequence to me? Could I have truly lived this long and been this ignorant?

What has transpired for me, within me, as I reconsider

this menagerie of people, are the threads that connect us. On any given day, the number of people who somehow brush up on the edges of my life or vice versa. Even if it's through media, the pages of a newspaper, the sound of their voice on the radio, these are people who I've been—and who I am.

Little by little I'm realizing the importance and the benefits of those connections, however brief or momentary, and forgetting to worry so much about people not receiving me well. Before now, I was so concerned about what people thought of me, of how strange I might appear to them, that I was missing a very important fact. Being offered a prayer is being offered a gift. There are days upon days where I don't have much to offer, but this little bit seems to be just what so many people needed as they were taking one more order or making change. I see it in the eyes of appreciation, connection, recognition, and remembrance. Somewhere along the way in the middle of all those few seconds, I'm making the world a better place.

ONCE UPON A TIME

**Prayer is not merely an occasional impulse
to which we respond when we are in trouble:
prayer is a life attitude.**

—WALTER A. MUELLER

HE WAS SITTING UP ON AN OLD LOG, WEARING A WHITE
T-shirt, sweat pouring down his face, but he was in
a state of cooling off. I had passed him on my way up the
walking trail in this part of the woods where I live. It was
once a railroad a long time ago. Then it became just much
of nothing. Then it was turned into a park, a rails to trails
program that cleared the brush and paved the rails much
to the delight of bikers, walkers, and general nature lovers.

What I enjoy most about this place, other than the tall
birds at the water's edge, the little railroad bridges that still
cover that span of waters here and there, the rock over-
hangs, or tiny waterfalls, are the people. More specifically,
I love the wide variety of people whom I discover here. I'm

not in my hurry-up, rush-rush mode. A part of me finds
my better side along the trees and animals scurrying, my
big white dog at my side. He and I are both happy among
the trees, a few minutes to relax and unwind. To say hello to
passing strangers, old people on bikes that haven't seen the
light of day for twenty years are suddenly riding them as far
as their legs will carry, little children running alongside. It's
a funny sight. Then there are big, burly guys with tattoos
walking with their women, Boy Scouts in troops, people
who arrive in special vans, assisted for the long walk. It's a
veritable menagerie of the finest kind. And in the middle of
this I am often at my best, willing to slow down and speak
a few minutes, to listen to a story, to pause as I am walking
past someone and wish them well, share with him or her
that I am praying. Of course sometimes, other times, I am
intent on making it to the next bridge or listening to a song
on my iPod and I pass someone just a little too quickly.

Such was the case with the older man in the white
T-shirt. I knew that when we passed each other in opposite
directions, him walking one way and me jogging the other.
I kept up my pace and let the man get away from me. But
when I turned around and made it back to the end of that
side of the trail where my car was parked, there he was. Sitting pretty as you please. I was delighted and decided right
then and there it was time to pause a little while and to
carry on a conversation.

Jim Kelly is his name and he walks this trail a few times

a week to stay in shape. He pats his stomach and laughs a little. "Shape" is a relative term, but he is working on his heart. "Had a heart attack not so long ago." Now, he's trying to keep the ticker working. Lost his wife four years ago, too. Nobody is doing too good, but he's been out walking.

He points to my dog. "That there one of those sheep dogs, isn't it?"

"Sheep and goats," I tell him. "They usually guard them out in the field." I pat Titan on his big, worthless head. "He doesn't guard anything but the sofa and watches too much Animal Planet."

"Oh, my." He's laughing and patting his stomach again. "He sure is a big thing."

"That he is. Big old baby. Thinks he's a lapdog, too." I point through the trees and down the trail. "You ever made it all the way to the end?" I ask him. "To the other side of the trail and back?"

"Been to the end?" He laughs at the absurdity of the thought of never seeing the other end of that track. "I reckon I have been to the end and back a few hundred times. I worked on the railroad back when they were laying the tracks. I've been around here forever." And so he has. Forever and a day maybe. I wonder what it's like to possess history that way. To be a part of something being carved out of the earth, bridges built, trains running, and then to walk on the ground that plows it all under in due progress.

We talk about that progress for a while, about the industries that have come and gone in this little place in middle Tennessee, about the economy and how people are getting by these days. Then I realize I really do have to be getting home to tasks that are waiting for me.

"I do this thing, Jim Kelly. I say prayers for somebody every day and today you're my person."

"Well, now, that's mighty fine."

"I'll be thinking about you and your heart and your walking."

He looks up into the trees and then back at me and says, "My sister Dorothy could use some prayer. She's not doing too good and she's still smoking and I try to tell her she better quit."

"And she's not listening to you?"

"No, she's not listening. She's on oxygen and she's still smoking!"

"Well, I used to smoke. It's a hard monkey to get off your back, that's for sure. You take care now, Jim Kelly."

"You, too, and take care of that big baby of yours."

I wish somehow at the end of the year I could gather all the people I've met along the way into one big room. I would like to see their faces again, not just in the unexpected corners of my mind where they turn up, but in person. I'd like for them to meet one another, for us to somehow exchange phone numbers just in case there came a time that one person might need another. I'd like for Jim Kelly to meet Peggy the diamond-wearing lady, and for them both to meet the young Muslim girl, Faith. For Gus and Pearl to meet Jewel.

A few years ago when my husband and I traveled to Italy, we met a man in Lucca who barely spoke English but he kept trying to explain to us that there was going to be a big party in the square and that we were invited, that we should be there.

"It's a party for all the peoples." He kept telling us, "All the peoples!" and stressing *All*. This is the party I want to have, one for all the peoples. And if there should be a place called heaven, I think this is what it will look like—a party for all the peoples. And we will be so happy to see one another as if we have been missing each other for a very long time. Strangers and friends, one and all.

Everything Matters

Prayer requires more of the heart than of the tongue.

—ADAM CLARKE

S HE WAS SITTING ALONE BY THE WINDOW OF A THAI RESTAU-
rant. I had carried a novel in with me, planned to eat
alone over the words, needing some time to relax and gather
my thoughts. The need is real, but perhaps I should learn to
do it another way. Or at least you would think by now, after
days upon days, months upon months, that I would at least
be sensitive to the moment. Open to other people when
I'm "out in the world." It doesn't always happen that way.
Sometimes, it's like a light switch because I can be so open,
so available on a given day or at the right moment, and then
like so many people, I can shut down. Like the lights aren't
on. But I seriously don't think we are supposed to live that
way. I don't, but sometimes I feel like I'm fighting against
my nature.

So, I walked into that Thai restaurant determined to eat

alone and speak to no one. And the minute I pass through the door, there is a woman sitting alone by the window. Her eyes literally light up when she sees me, as if she recognizes me or was waiting on me. As if we are old friends or new buddies. She had such a nice smile and an expression that said, "Finally, you're here!" And I walked right past her, sat at another table along the window, ordered, and put my head down in the book.

It's always after the fact that I get this; my retrospect is so crystal clear. I could have actually said—oh, stop the traffic—I could have asked her if she'd like to join me. And even writing those words, I can feel the shell around me cracking into fine irretraceable lines. I know I am not and cannot be everyone's best friend. I know I have difficulty just squeezing in time for my family. But there are moments when I think—no, know—that I should try to make more of a connection. So every person I pray for can't become someone I speak with by phone every week—although you'd be amazed at how often I wish that could be the case. I really want to stay in contact. I want to find out what's going on with Gloria, Nadine, Gus, and all the others out there. And in spite of that I sit with cold eyes, face to book, back to woman. Why, why, why?

Even if I had just said, *Hi, do I know you?* And then followed up with, *Well, my name is River and nice to meet you,* the world wouldn't have stopped. Even if I hadn't invited myself to sit down with her, perhaps that old pickup line,

"Don't I know you from somewhere?" could have connected us.

I never felt like that woman was necessarily "the person"
I was supposed to pray for. I just felt like I was unfriendly
to a complete stranger when I had the opportunity to be
otherwise. My back burned so bad with an awareness of her
presence and my determination not to connect with her
that I finally did turn around. She was gone.

Eventually, another woman came in alone, took the seat
at the table directly behind me. I went out of my way when
I was leaving to say something to her. To comment on what
she was reading and to say have a nice day. She wasn't recep-
tive at all. Just kind of grunted and went back to her book.

It's okay, I thought. *I know you because I'm just like you.*

Me trying to speak to her didn't make up for the woman
with the expectant eyes that I had cold-shouldered. All I can
say is this: I had to fight myself to keep from turning around
and speaking to her. Part of me really wanted to keep to
myself, but there was another part that was nudging me
out of my comfort zone. I know that was a result of this
year and the kinds of responses I've received, the realization
of what it can mean, what it might matter, to someone just
to speak to them. And that bothersome pit in my stomach
where lunch didn't settle so well? It's all due to me having
more of a connected conscience. Whatever peace I have
on this situation is this: The worry and the bother are new
things, and I'll take that as a good sign.

The Face of Love

Prayers go up and blessings come down.

—YIDDISH PROVERB

I HAD BEEN WORKING IN PARTHENON PARK IN NASHVILLE this morning. There is liquid-fast wi-fi, a beautiful little lake, weeping willows that sweep the water's edge, and always a gaggle of geese that make this place their year-round home. The Parthenon looms large, a strange shadow of another civilization and a land that is somewhere else. It is very out of place in a Southern city that embraces this leftover life-size replica from the Tennessee Centennial and International Exposition fair of 1897. Now dances fill the park, movies on summer nights, dog shows, artisan fairs, and photographer exhibits. People walk and jog its manicured paths and gardens, picnic on its green lawns, and stroll babies through the flowers.

It was one of the first places I came to visit when I moved to Nashville. I toured the inside of the Parthenon, pored over the old state fair photographs, and saw an incredible exhibit featuring women during the Depression. Tourists come to visit the Parthenon every day, but I can tell you it's a city park. The locals claim it and keep it as their own.

Now I am a local, writing from my car, watching the fountains. Occasionally, I glance up at the puppies on parade, people jogging with their dogs, families, and walkers. People really are the most varied, the most amazing wonders of the world. Then I glance up and see a young boy with what I suppose might be cerebral palsy. A young man is with him, pushing the wheelchair. I watch a moment and then I look back down to work. The next time I look up, it appears the man is struggling with the boy, moving him or lifting him, and he seems to sit him down roughly in the wheelchair. My hand flies to the door handle, my other hand reaching for my cell phone. If this child is being abused, I will not let that man get away unreported or the abused uncomforted. I continue watching. I see the man saying something; the boy's head falls back and then to the side as he responds. I save my work, close the laptop, and pick up my cell phone again.

The memory of that boy at the ski resort from months ago is right there, shimmering on the surface. I want somehow to save him by saving this boy. Is he being abused? Is the man being rough? Are his words unfriendly? I'm an imperfect bystander, a windshield away and out of earshot of the truth.

The man pushes the chair over to the water's edge. I tap my fingers on the steering wheel, watching, waiting for something I can't put my finger on. For evidence of wrong-doing, ready to rush forward if I need to. He pulls out food for the geese and then the flock moves slowly through the water, toward the man and the boy, and I relax a little. "Lifting him," I say aloud, "he was only lifting him, rearranging him."

Then I feel bad for my suspicion. I've held six-month-old babies that wore my back out. Surely, caring for someone of considerably larger size, moving him, rearranging him, is taxing. But I'm still watching just to make sure. When you decide to rescue someone, it's hard to let go. The man is walking on the rocks at the water's edge in front of the boy, and then he slowly lifts his arm out to his side, and begins to flap them wildly. The geese follow suit; they flap and call to one another. He flaps faster and jumps down from the rocks and begins to run around the boy's wheelchair, flapping and squawking, and the boy is laughing so hard the man starts laughing, too. Then he falls down on the grass next to the boy's wheelchair and they are both still laughing. But not me. I'm not laughing at all. I'm sitting there behind the wheel crying because I witnessed this thing. This moment of what looked like love in its purest, rarest, most valuable form. I loved that man in that moment with all my heart. That kind of love called agape, the kind that transcends stuff and things. The kind we are supposed to aspire to but have such a horribly hard time wrapping our fingers around. I prayed for a heart like that. For the man and, yes, the boy, but also for me to have a heart that raised its arms wide, and ran with full-out silly wonderful for the sake of anyone.

TELLER TIME

**Look for God. Look for God like a man
with his head on fire looks for water.**

—ELIZABETH GILBERT

SOMETIMES MY BRAVERY SURPRISES ME. IF THAT SOUNDS LIKE a prideful statement, I don't mean for it to. Some days, many days, I say prayers and blessings for people and never tell them. Other days, I tell hesitantly or brush past people and tell them as quickly as I can. Other days, like this day, I'm a strange product of determination.

I'd been asked to run an errand for my husband. We bank at separate banks for no particular reason; this is just the way that things worked out. While he may carefully study interest rates, bank charges, and hidden fees before he signs up, I'm more likely to join the bank giving out tote bags or free popcorn.

This day I'm standing in a teller line taking care of business for my husband and I'm looking around, glancing at strangers, when the woman in a glass-partitioned office catches my attention. And holds it. She's with a customer, and when I finish with my transactions, I go stand near her door. Another bank employee approaches me and asks me very kindly if she can assist me.

"No, thanks, I need to see that woman right there."

"Oh, Marion. Okay, it may be a while."

"It's okay, I'll wait for her."

It is a while. She is carefully going over someone's statement with him, line item by line item. I thumb through some magazine that isn't anything I would ever buy or read and wonder how I have managed to leave the house without a book in my purse. Eventually, Marion stands and sees her customer to the door, says her good-byes, and then turns to me.

"Come in, come in. Now how can I help you today?"

"Well, really . . ." How many different ways can I begin this story? "I was here just running an errand for my husband."

"Sit down, sit down."

"And I have this resolution that I have had all year. It's the only one I've never broken."

In my mind, she is slowly reaching beneath the desk for the red button. The one designed for emergencies and carrying crazy people out of the bank.

"I pray for a stranger every day. Not, like, in person. I think about them all day and before I go to sleep."

"How nice."

I figure her fingers have just about pressed the alarm at this point.

"And today you're my person and that's all I have to say. I just wanted to tell you that." I stand up to go.

"Do you bank with us?" She reaches for her business card.

"No, ma'am, not for any particular reason I just ended up elsewhere."

"Well, you should consider opening an account. I've been here fifteen years."

"Yes, ma'am. I may do that on another day." I look at her card and stand there just for a second. "Anything special maybe you'd like prayer for?"

Marion's voice drops down a few notches and it turns to a soft velvet. The bank loses her for just a moment as real life seeps in. "Yes. My husband—he has cancer. It's not good."

Sometimes a face can say all it needs to. There are great gifts called compassion and a face that can express it. I'm seriously saddened by this news.

"Forty-two years we've been married," she says.

She doesn't look that old but that dignity, the way she carries herself, the way she speaks even of these times of trouble, I imagine that's the kind of thing that comes with age. A surety in the face of all trials. A confidence from secret places, aged places to draw upon in times of trouble.

"Forty-two years is a good amount of time," I tell her. "That's a lot of stories right there."

"It sure is that. A whole lot of stories." That's with a quick smile, perhaps a twinge of humor at a quick memory, but then she is back to the business at hand. "He's very, very sick."

"I understand. And I'll be praying for you and your husband."

"I appreciate that. He surely needs it." She rises and shakes my hand. "And you should remember what I told you now. Come back and see me about that account."

I pull out of the parking lot thinking about Marion and her husband. About that part about how long they had been married, sleeping side by side. About the vows about for better or for worse, in sickness and in health, and till death do us part. And about how sometimes standing around and waiting for a stranger is worth it.

HOME SWEET HOME

**If you can't pray as you want to, pray as you can.
God knows what you mean.**

—VANCE HAVNER

*H*OME. THAT WORD, THAT PLACE, THAT CONCEPT, HAS BEEN the subject of so many requests this year. Personally, I always equate home to the word *safe.* When the hobbits finally make it safely back to the Shire, they're home again. When my favorite baseball team makes it safely around all the bases, they've made it home. A lot of family traditions or church traditions involve a homecoming day, and many of us consider the afterlife a type of going home. One of my favorite songs by singer Marc Broussard is simply titled "Home," a great rocking tune about that baby boy getting on the bus and making it back to see his mama, and Eva Cassidy sang about going home to see her mama and daddy as well. *Home*—the concept is so deeply embedded in us that the simple word conjures up images of what we fight to protect and long to return to. Be it the mother country or Grandma's house, or a house we've yearned to purchase for years, we have a place inside of us that represents the good life. Even those of us who may gypsy around in life or can move on a dime have someone or something that represents security, the touchable place where all good things from lives are kept, and where the door will always open wide upon our arrival.

Angela, my stranger one day, whom I met in a hospital lunch break room while I was waiting on my sister, asks me to please pray for their home to be refinanced. "My husband's hours have been cut back so much and we're trying to save our house." She is amazingly hopeful. Still she asks for a little extra prayer cover. "We have to get the refinancing to make it work." Her hopefulness is contagious and I'm so hoping right along with her that the bank, the mortgage company, the lender whoever they might be, will help her keep what belongs to her.

It's been a year like that, me hoping with so many people in this predicament. So many people trying to save their homes or who are beyond that. Who are trying to get over the heartbreak of having already lost theirs.

Madeline is standing in a department store when I approach her and say very quietly my entire—what should I call it now? Routine? That's not right. It means so much more than that. I remain very hesitant about approaching people. And the prayers are even more heartfelt than I'm conveying here.

"Thanks, I appreciate that. I'll pray for you, too." She's just a little reserved. I don't blame her, not a bit.

I tell her thanks and begin to walk away but then I return. "Is there anything, I don't know . . . special that you'd like prayer for?" It's a bold question to me but it's asked so hesitantly it's a wonder the words don't vaporize from my mouth before they reach her.

She pauses before she answers. Not because she doesn't have a request ready, because I can see she does. I can see the way her eyes pinch down harder like an old headache has resurfaced. "Yes," she says softly. Then she begins to tell me the story. About her or her husband losing their jobs, perhaps it was both of them. That part I can't get straight in my memory. What I do know is the rest of the request after she tells me how they lost their house, how they tried their best to keep it but in the end nothing could stop the process. "We're okay, really. Me and my husband, that is. We found a trailer and moved the family. So all in all, we're okay. We're going to be all right."

I can see that this part is true. I see the survivor in her, the backbone toughness of getting along and getting by. She wouldn't be quick to ask for help or a handout from any-one. Not her closest neighbor.

"But my son," she says, "Daniel. For him it's not so easy at all. He's twelve. It's a tough age, you know. He left his friends behind and went through . . . everything when we lost the house. We were in a neighborhood."

"Daniel," I repeat and commit his name, his age to memory. "I understand a boy that age. I have sons. They've really been through some tough times, too."

She has visibly softened from the first moment I spoke to her and even now I can still see her face, still see her standing there in the merchandise, wandering in a way, distracting her mind from trouble, having a little quiet time. I know about the need for that, too. When trouble drives you to seek quiet comfort.

I think of Daniel periodically throughout the day and later at night, considering the way of boys, of children, of the knocks and changes that we endure becoming people. And then I think of Madeline and know how much a son's safety and happiness weigh on a mother's heart. Yes, I do understand.

MUDDY MEET-UPS

**I believe that prayer is our powerful contact
with the greatest force in the universe.**

—LORETTA YOUNG

M Y NEPHEW IS PLAYING SOCCER. WELL, IT'S SUPPOSED TO be soccer, but it has turned into a huge mud pit with small, sliding five-year-olds careening into one another. They've never had so much permission to get this filthy. You can't even recognize one child from the other. It's kind of fun and kind of horrible and ridiculous. It's tournament day so there are these mud pit contests going on all over the field. Orange markers are sticking out of the ground so that you can determine where the field is supposed to be.

"This is insane," I tell my sister. "Why didn't they cancel this until next week?"

"I don't know but they didn't. That other team is playing; see that field way over there?" she asks, pointing to a mud pit six mud pits beyond this one we're currently standing in.

"There are no fields," I tell her. "There is just a mess. A big, whopping, squishy mess. Just look at my shoes."

My sister looks down with a discerning eye. "I can't see your shoes."

"That's my point." I have on running shoes that are two years old. They haven't seen enough running to be worn out, but today's event may be the end of them.

It begins to rain. "I can't take this anymore," I say as I turn to go and search for my car in the tournament's crowded parking lot.

"Where are you going?"

"To get rubber mud boots."

"But it's almost over."

"It was over before it started but nobody noticed and I can't walk, but I'll be back." I'm not a tomboy but I'm not a serious girlie-girl either. I love looking at clothes but I have well established that I don't love shopping for them. Today is an exception. I've never wanted to shop for something so much in all my life—rubber boots that come up to my knees.

I rush just a few miles over the speed limit to the nearest Seed and Feed store where surely said boots will be lined up near the door and waiting. Closed! Now, I need to rush a little faster to make it to the closest store to procure said items. I assure you that I wouldn't go to this trouble for normal mud, not a rainy day, a little wet ground, a little slosh. I grew up spending childhood summers on the creek in the woods. I know mud. But today, well, this is the kind you get after a three-day flood where the creek rises and sits still for days on end. And the kids are playing in it. My only other option would have been to roll up my pants, take off my shoes, and walk barefoot. But it's also cold. Not happening.

Park, park, park. Hurry, hurry, hurry. To the back of the big-box store where along the wall there are boots. Big, luscious knee-high rubber boots. I grab a pair closest to my size and turn to go so I can hurry, hurry, hurry back and hope my nephew hasn't noticed I'm missing. But then I notice a woman in the shoe aisle and freeze cartoon-style midstep. Sigh. Step back, back, back.

"Hi there, you don't know me but . . ." and so it begins again.

"Holly," she tells me. "I sure do appreciate that. My husband died about six months ago so I'm alone."

"I'm sorry." I balance my weight, move the boots to the other hand, and wait for Holly to tell me what she needs to and there's no exact time limit on that. "That changes things for you."

"I have to do everything now." She looks down in her shopping cart but keeps waiting. I know her shopping list isn't what's on her mind. "You never realize before just how much you talk about things, you know? About how you make decisions together. Now I have to do everything and think about everything. It's not easy."

"I'm sure it's not. My mother has gone through that. Daddy passed away a few years ago so she's had to keep everything going on her own. She says it's funny how the little things would trip her up. Small decisions, you know, that they used to make together."

"That's true, the little things. And that I have to do everything. It's not easy," she says again. Then she adds how much she wants to thank me and gives me a hug before I hurry away.

As quick as I can, I'm back in the car, ripping off the soggy shoes and pulling on the boots. Back on the soccer field or what was once upon a time a soccer field, I find my sister on the far backside mud pit. The game is over and the kids are rushing around in circles, then sliding in the mud.

"It's over," she says.

"Did he miss me?"

"No, don't think he noticed. They're giving out end-of-the-year trophies next."

So I missed the final game where my nephew may or may not have scored a goal. I did capture pictures of the trophy award ceremony and him covered in brown sludge. His big sister, all of eight and quite the fashionista, was appropriately impressed with the boots. She believes in dressing correctly for all occasions.

In the middle of all the mayhem, rain, mud, and the day's confusion, I was able to meet a stranger. Maybe I was meant to have a sudden craving for rubber boots that would lead me to the back of the store just in time to meet Holly. To listen to her story and to let her know that someone hears her, someone who realizes it is indeed not easy in this world being on your own. Someone who is offering up a prayer on her behalf.

I believe in these kinds of meetings, in strange circumstances where people cross our paths for a reason. I've had too many experiences like this one not to.

ALIENS IN PARADISE

I believe in prayer and in strong belief.

—TINA TURNER

I T'S COLD AND RAINING IN NASHVILLE. NASHVILLE IS A PLACE pretty far south, and that might bring with it a few images of warm, blue skies, and blooming flowers. Today isn't that kind of day. It's the kind of cold, drizzly day that can soak into your bones. The kind where the sky is one big gray blanket sitting down on the city. The kind I imagine that is perfect for leaving some people cold and lonely. When I pass the boy, I keep on walking, coat tied tight, hood pulled up. But it's not too many steps before I turn around and go back to him. He's working with a landscape crew of about eight men that I can see. They are setting out trees, each of them digging holes that are about twelve feet away from each other.

"Do you mind if I ask your name?"

He is hesitant, looks over my shoulder at another one of the men. Then I get it.

"You're not in trouble. I just want to know your name because"—I pause—"do you understand me?"

Communication is the key. It's what surrounds our days and dreams. Symbols and imaginings, real words, old letters, inferred or spoken thoughts. As a young woman in the early fifties, my mother had moved to Miami. Still in the same state she was born and raised in, it was a far cry from the backwoods of Northern Florida. It was nothing less than a tropical paradise to her. Many years later when I was a little girl, when life's circumstances found us living with my father where he was stationed in Amberg, Germany, she would tell me, "Someday I'm going to take you to Miami." She painted pictures for me of the palm trees, warm breezes, and perpetual pink of flowers unfolding. When I was five years old, it became a dream of mine as well. A Southern girl trapped in the cold, gray skies of a German morning, missing her grandmother and all the things she considered good—which are things associated with Florida and warm places—would say, "Mama," pulling at her from whatever chore she was busy with. "When are we going to your ami?"

"What? Going where?"

"Your ami, Mama. With the pink flowers."

"No, no." She crouched down on one knee so we'd be eye to eye, all the better to make her point. "It's not my ami—it's Miami."

"That's what I said. When are we going to your ami?"

This riddling question and answer went on for a number of years, with me never understanding how my mama's *ami*, as I referred to it, didn't actually belong to her and her alone. It was also several years before we did indeed take a trip to Miami, where things had changed a lot but she could still point out Flagler Street and the places where she had walked to work. The palms were everything she promised, the pink flowers profuse, and I can see why it was a place of wonder to her all those years ago.

"I never could get you to understand what I was trying to tell you." We were eating black beans and plantains. "It just about drove me crazy."

"Sometimes we just can't communicate, Mom. We weren't speaking the same language."

Now, I'm staring this boy in the face, asking if he understands me. I might as well be telling him about Miami. He's just a kid, I tell you. Sixteen maybe. He nods a little. I touch his arm gently. "You're not in trouble," I say again but then I realize I need to add, "with me." And I'm thinking he's not going to understand the word *resolution*. All my good words, the things I was going to say, that I normally say, well, they're just no good here in this situation.

"Prayers for you. God bless you. You understand." I'm trying desperately to remember unused Spanish twenty years old. All I can think of are old Western movies set on the border and *vaya con Dios*. "Dios," I say. "*Mucho gusto tu*, Francisco. *Vaya con Dios.*"

Well, that makes no sense, I think, but he stands in the rain and smiles. Okay. So maybe he gets a little of it.

"Sí, sí," he says and smiles tentatively. I pat his arm and turn around thinking I might want to brush up on my Spanish. And I get the weirdest sense of longing as I begin to walk away. I turn around again and watch him digging in the rain.

"He misses his mama," I say to no one nearby. The wind picks up and whips my hood off as I turn back and walk inside where it's warm and order a coffee. That boy misses his mama. And that is something pretty universal that I can understand beyond borders and confusion about laws and what's best or not best, what's right and not right. I can understand the mother part. And wherever she is, I'm betting his mother is missing him, too. Maybe they have shared stories. Maybe they have made plans to see paradise.

"Vaya con Dios, indeed, Francisco."

BACK ALLEYS AND WELL-WISHES

There comes a time when a person just has to do what his heart, what his soul tell him to do.

—JACK REED

WE ALL GET INSPIRATION WHERE WE FIND IT. SOME FROM television, some from books, or role models. Oftentimes for me it is from the strangest street people, who respond to me in such ways that they open my eyes to something brand-new. They help me look at life in a new light. This is one of the things that I've treasured most about my year of meeting and reaching out to strangers—it's not how I'm affecting them that matters most, it's how they are affecting me.

I've had these experiences in the past. I haven't been immune to them, but my contact with people hasn't been so frequent or direct. It's been happenstance, and as it so happens, those encounters have often been with people on the streets.

A few years ago now, I had been studying for finals at a donut shop where I took up residence as often as I could, drained their coffeepots that had free refills, and studied with just enough stimulation to keep me awake but not distract me. On one particular day, I had studied for hours, then packed up my bags and gone to my car. When I pulled around to the rear of the store to exit the parking lot, I saw a man rummaging through the Dumpster for food. The sight of this affected me so greatly that I stopped, rolled down the window, and called him over. I took out a folded twenty-dollar bill and passed it to him. Now, twenty dollars when I was a young mother returning to school was more than a lot. But it's what I had and it's what I felt moved to give. I know there was a chance that this man was a bum, a drug user, or chose a life of living on the streets when other options were open to him. That wasn't the point at the moment. What was imperative was that I act with grace, that I take action regarding the thing that had moved me. That all logical reasons not to bless the man with twenty dollars be washed aside for the moment because maybe there really was a traceable chain of events that had brought him to this place.

The man came to the car window and I passed him the folded-up bill. Dirt streaked his face and hands but not too badly, all things considered. But then this is what happened and this is why it's still in my memory, and why it comes to mind so many years later:

His eyes lit up from the inside. I don't mean that in a movie-special-effects kind of way, not even in the way that wonderfully strange things happen in my novels. I mean it in the way that the light in someone's soul can suddenly shine a little brighter and the eyes seem to be the very place that light breaks loose and shines most.

"And how are *you* today?" he asked me with such genuine interest, with such empathy, that as far as I was concerned, he could have been Jesus in the flesh.

Me? How am I? I had this incredulous feeling of *how could anything possibly be wrong with me?* After all, I'm not foraging in Dumpsters for food. But the way he asked it, the sincerity in his voice and face, caused my heart to jump and tears to spring to my eyes. *I don't really know,* I wanted to say. *I'm not sure I can tell you, honest-to-goodness and down-to-the-bone, exactly how I am, but thank you, thank you for actually asking.*

And then I realize that's the key. How often are we really touched by the sincerity of the question, of someone asking and really wanting to know exactly how we are? I think it's a rare occurrence, even with spouses and family and the closest of friends. The flipside of the coin, of course, is how often are we asking the people closest to us how they are and really taking the time then to listen?

Months and months of introducing myself to strangers and basically telling them, *I care how you are. Is there anything special you're going through? Anything special you need prayer for?* has made it perfectly clear that people aren't getting these questions often enough. It's why people are so taken by surprise, or refreshed, or so touched. It's a hungry world out there. People are starving for one single touch, a breath of a prayer. It's really not too much to ask.

UNINTERRUPTED

**A prayer in its simplest definition
is merely a wish turned Godward.**

—PHILLIPS BROOKS

W E HAVE SOMEHOW CREATED A SOCIETY IN WHICH WE don't often get involved, we look the other way, and we think someone else will fill a particular need or step up in some wonderful altruistic way. Someday we cross that line and surprise ourselves by being someone's hero, their confidant, and their friend in passing. Other days, we walk on by. The reasons are not always selfish or self-serving. Sometimes we don't want to intrude, to hurt someone's feelings in the process, to overstep our bounds, to be a nuisance, to be a know-it-all . . . the list goes on as life goes by and we continue walking past people who possibly needed us.

Just the other day I was walking out the doors of a major store to my car. There at the front of the parking lot was an elderly gentleman, parked in the handicapped zone, and struggling somewhat to move a woman who I assumed was his wife from a wheelchair to the front seat of the car. I wanted to help but I didn't. I did whisper a prayer that he manage the best that he could. I slowed down in my walking, I hesitated at my car, and I considered rushing back to where they were.

My hesitation was genuine. I didn't want to embarrass the man. In a flash my imagination filled in everything that I didn't know about them. They'd been married over fifty years with one of those stop-the-presses, award-winning unions. The kind where he was indeed her hero, her knight in shining armor. I didn't want to embarrass them. I didn't want for him to appear weak or for me to appear strong. So I didn't interrupt them, but I did pray heartily for him to get her in that car easily. To get her safely out again when they made it home and into the house without having a heart attack himself in the process. And for them to get all the help they might need, which is pretty ironic since I could have been the one who was the answer to that prayer but wasn't.

What I needed was the brilliant honesty, the unafraid, curious honesty of my youngest son, who had accompanied me to the post office when he was almost four years old. A man came in wearing a short-sleeved shirt, but there was one thing different about him, which my son picked up on right away. The man only had one arm, the other missing from somewhere near the shoulder. My son, never being one to mince words or to shy away from a direct conversation, pointed to the missing limb and in a loud, clear voice asked, "Where's your arm?" I tried to explain to him that such questions were not polite. The man actually corrected me, telling me it was normal for a child to be curious and to step right up and ask questions. Then, if I remember correctly, he went on to tell my son that lions had ripped it off when he was on safari hunting wild game in the jungle or some such thing, which was completely plausible to a four-year-old boy.

Yes, I should have stopped. I didn't have to point to missing extremities, only to address the fact that they were struggling. I have experience at this with a history of growing up with grandparents in the home, with aging relatives, with my daddy finally passing away at home. I understand the process that sometimes seasons on this earth can take. And yes, my human need not to be embarrassed by them or for them held me back from doing what is right.

I should have gone back. I should have been less concerned that my assistance would be taken as intrusion, realizing they could have accepted the help gladly or told me to buzz off. Receiving or rejecting then would have been their option and responsibility, but offering in the first place, stepping up to offer help, lend a hand—that was all in my court. Prayers are worth so very much, but at the same time they are not a substitute for getting involved, however momentary that involvement may be. Maybe they are just a good beginning. A prayer well intentioned that leads to us recognizing moments where we are called to become more involved with the needs we encounter both on a small scale—like right there in the parking lot—or on a larger one—for example, aiding a country suffering from a disaster. Becoming involved will always require something of us. What we get in return, either the appreciation or the simple knowledge that we did the right thing, is an unexpected sweet reward.

MAPQUEST

To be a Christian without prayer is no more possible than to be alive without breathing.

—MARTIN LUTHER KING, JR.

I WALK INTO A LOCAL SHIPPING SERVICE CENTER LOOKING FOR directions. I figure if they can't find an address, I'll give up. The guy behind the counter is the only one in the place. It's very early yet; maybe about the time he just unlocked the doors. I'm just there for directions, but immediately I know I need to share my other tidbit of news. Daryl helps me map out my destination just like I was certain that he could. I tell him thank you but then I'm standing there hesitating, procrastinating.

"Is there anything else we can help you with today?" He smiles and waits patiently.

"Well, yes, kind of, Daryl." I say, pointedly looking at the name on his tag.

"How is that?"

"Well, I do this thing where I pray for somebody every day."

"Ohhh, I see."

He may have taken a little step back away from the counter that separates us. And I'm thinking he thinks I'm a nutcase or that I'm going to jump over that counter and lay hands on him suddenly or pray that he sees the light of day. One of those my-way-or-the-highway kind of prayers.

"So." I take a step toward the door as I continue talking. I think he visibly relaxes. "I'll be praying for you as I go about my day, you know. Just be thinking good things for you. Say a prayer for you before I fall asleep and all that."

I don't think prayer is a two-bit exercise in futility. I don't think it's lightweight or inconsequential. My trying to explain how I intend to pray for people in a light-handed way isn't to demean what I hope is the true significant substance of those prayers. What I am so serious about is that they realize I am not trying to convert or condemn them but just to offer a prayer to help them get on in this life.

Daryl is watching me as I put my hand on the door and get ready to make my exit.

"I see," he says. "Thanks."

"Anything special then you'd like me to pray for while I'm about it?"

"Yes, yes, I would." He has stepped back toward the counter now, his hands resting on the surface. "My dad."

He pauses and looks away. "He just had a heart attack. He sure could use prayer."

I take my hand off the door, slow my whole, entire self down a little. No, a lot. Suddenly I'm not afraid that Daryl is going to think I'm obtrusive or crazy or some kind of fanatic that has come walking in here to trick him or pass judgment on him. He knows I'm for real. He continues.

"And my mom 'cause she has had a bunch of ministrokes so she hasn't been doing so good."

God bless him. Here he is in uniform, this seriously grown man, strong enough to lift big things and hoof them around up and down hills, trucks, and driveways all day but his heart for his mother and father is as pure as a baby's.

We talk just a few minutes about his parents and how they've been doing or not doing. His dad just got out of the hospital, has just come home, but everything has been a little scary, a little touch-and-go. On an ordinary day where I just go in to try to get directions, not so suddenly, and very deliberately, I'm having a conversation with the stranger behind the counter. In the process I'm making a connection that's just a little more than something superficial in passing.

THE ARTISAN

Intercessory prayer might be defined as
loving our neighbour on our knees.

—CHARLES BRENT

T HE FIRST THING I REALLY NOTICE WHEN I PASS THIS
menagerie is that they are beautiful. There are birdhouses of every size carved and fashioned into shape. A man
stands out there with his hands in his pockets, smiling and
talking to a potential customer. His family, the whole lot of
them, is in or around the pickup truck. There's the wife and
three, four, or five children. I'm not certain if they all belong
to him or if friends of the children have jumped aboard for
the day's outing. He has set up a temporary shop in the
parking lot of another store, displaying his wares proudly to
people who might stop and invest a little time and money.

I drove by once, but before I could park, I turned around
and went back, parked my car, and got out. The tough
financial times have continued to travel up this way. But

for all practical purposes, poor people in the rural South have been used to tough times for generations. What happens or doesn't happen in the stock market doesn't have the same effect as it might on a million other families. I once asked my mother how the Great Depression affected them. I wanted to know what happened when everything crashed. "We were always depressed," she said. "We never knew the difference." There's always the eventual trickle-down but I guess they were too close to the bottom to ever feel a thing.

I'm guessing that no matter where the trickle-down catches this Mr. Laramie Brown, who has just introduced himself to me, it will find him being busy, working at building something with his hands, and finding an open spot to sell it. He's going to find a way to be industrious in hard times using the only material he can find and what he knows how to do.

We get to talking, and although I should be rushing to get a few last-minute ingredients for guests coming to dinner, I have to stop and visit for a while. I have to tell him, *Today you are my stranger.*

He smiles.

I look over the back of the truck. "Sir"—I point to the houses—"you are a true artist."

"Oh, thank you thank you." His words come out fast and rolled together, becoming one long string to decipher and understand.

"These are incredibly beautiful." And they are. These

aren't those mass-produced birdhouses you buy at the store. They're handmade in different hues of wood, carved spirals gracing openings. I have to go but mentally I'm making a shopping list, thinking of people I can gift these wonderful creations to. "Do you have a phone number?"

Laramie gives me the number, which I scratch down on the back of another business card. I look over at the old truck, the children, the beautiful woodwork.

"I'll be thinking about you—wishing you all good things." And I will, but they won't be prayers for a desperate man. I think he told me he was a welder, had been a welder but the welders at the plant got laid off one by one, so that now, well, this is what he's got left. This is what he does. He's not desperate. Wouldn't call him a dreamer either. He's a provider, both a thinker and a doer. He's an entrepreneur. If he had a marketing plan and some great connection, he wouldn't be traveling around on this truck out in the sun. He'd be creating and other people would be doing all the selling. But maybe that isn't the point.

Personally, I don't think any prayers said out of due course of someone's life are suddenly heard. I believe prayers must match up with a person's heart and destiny. That's why praying for someone's blessings works for me, for true love and honest, good friends. Universal things, which are to me innate human desires and help us live a simple, happy life.

For all I know, Laramie's favorite part of this entire

process is loading that family up in the truck and driving around until they find the perfect spot. Then getting to see the faces of people up close appreciating the work his hands have produced. I don't need to pray that Laramie finds an investor, gets a dot-com. I just need to pray for all the blessings that he can have in this life to find their way to him, for his cup to overflow with grace and goodness, and for his family to be well fed, warm, and well.

It's such a simple thing, really. I also need to buy some birdhouses.

My Mother's Keeper

**The great people of the earth today are the people
who pray, (not) those who talk about prayer . . .
but I mean those who take time and pray.**

—S. D. GORDON

I'T'S HER COUGH THAT GETS MY ATTENTION. IT PULLS ME
straight out of my own thoughts, where I was lost in
consideration of a lot of details all surrounding immediate family members. But the cough overrules those
thoughts. It's constant, one of those hacking, rattling,
just won't stop coughs no matter what you do coughs.
I'm at a gas station, where I've set my pump to auto-fill
while I jump back into the warmth of the car and out of
the biting wind. I leave my window cracked just so I can
hear the telltale click when it shuts off, but what is getting my attention and keeping my attention is the sound
of that cough. *That would be my stranger for the day*, I think. I
get out of my car and follow the sound. The wind whips

around my hair, around my coat. I pull it tighter and round the pumps.

She's an elderly woman, pumping gas with those frail hands, the skin so thin it looks transparent. There's a fresh bruise on the back of her hand, and one on her arm above it. Older people are like that a lot. Easy to bruise, easy to bleed through the skin once bruised. My grandmother was like that. My mother is getting older. This fact amazes me actually. That she is the last living of her seven siblings. That time has marched on in her life. I see her as unconquerable, a survivor, as the strongest woman I've ever known. I've mentally locked her into an age younger than I am now and I think there must be a part of me that thinks she will live forever. But the fact is she's getting older, weaker. That she needs help for a lot of simple things that involve lifting and moving. And as I look at the woman standing frail, bruised, and windblown in the biting cold, I hope my mother is somewhere inside and that her car has a full tank.

I approach the woman gently, speaking softly. I really don't want to frighten her. "Need me to help pump that for you?"

"Oh, thank you, I have it started now. I'm okay."

I hang around, a little awkward, fighting the blustery gusts. It's really one of the windiest days we've ever had in Nashville. "I had one resolution this year," I tell her, "only one." I ask her name.

"Meredith." She smiles.

I share with her that I sure will be praying for her and wonder if that bruise on the back of her hand is from a stay in the hospital, caused by an IV needle stuck in the tender skin of a worn-out hand.

Or perhaps she tripped and fell. It has become one of my mother's greatest frustrations, this tripping and falling over seemingly nothing. Not too long ago, just stepping up on my sister's small porch carrying grocery bags, she had a really nasty fall and dislocated her shoulder. That's how quickly it can happen, two small plastic bags, two small steps, and months to recuperate.

I consider the Merediths of the world, the aged who are on their own, who have had to learn to get by on their own. They've had to learn to pump gas, which used to be unheard of, to self-scan, self-serve, and self-survive. In a society where we've stayed on the move, or just stayed away, how many millions struggle all on their own every day. I'm not sure this is the natural order of things.

"You need to maybe get home, Meredith. Maybe get out of this wind." She is the sweetest thing. Really, you can tell sometimes. The old people. I worry about them getting on and getting by in this world. My mother is states away, and although she is surrounded by people who care about her and my cousin lives twenty minutes away, I worry about her.

But here I am offering to pump gas for a woman in Tennessee, my cousin is swinging by my mother's to help her safely unload her car, and across the world, there are neighbors looking out for elderly neighbors. Maybe that's the answer. To realize that some grumpy old man on the block isn't just an isolated neighbor who makes you want to curse sometimes over his antics. It's someone's family—someone out there somewhere who's not coming around much or can't get there. Do we have a universal chance to step up to the plate? To sacrifice a little time for those who may be needing more help than their pride will let them admit? I think we do. I think the least I can do is say a little prayer as I'm passing by.

BIRTHDAYS IN
STRANGE LANDS

Prayer draws us near to our own souls.

—HERMAN MELVILLE

M Y COUSIN HAS WON A TRIP FOR TWO TO COSTA RICA. A
land of volcanoes and coffee beans, rain forests and
oceans. She's chosen me to travel with her for a number of
far-flung reasons, but she says it's for my birthday. She's gotten me into more trouble all of my life than any one single
person, and I know we will have an amazing time on this
adventure.

I packed my bags, my swimsuit, sweaters, and my resolution. I wouldn't be leaving it behind whether I could say
more than *Vaya con Dios* or not. If my prayers had to stay
silent and my strangers a mystery, so be it. I wouldn't stop
praying.

We traveled a few thousand miles by air, rode a shuttle

bus and then another bus that curved its way through foggy mountains. We are in the rain forest region now. The place of incredible vistas that spill out into valleys and rivers. The roads are notorious wayward bumps. My cousin assures me we will be staying in a lovely historic hotel downtown. I read the description and in between the lines.

"We'll be staying in an old dump of a place with no air and bars on the windows."

"No we won't," she assures me. "It says it's four stars."

I smile and look out the window at the scenery. "It's all right, it'll all be okay, I'm sure."

I'm actually not worried about where we're going. It really will be all right. I've traveled a lot in my life—to places that are beautiful and luxurious and to those that are off the beaten track and maybe a little worn down from wear. I know not to walk the streets at night alone and how to make a barricade of all the furniture in the room. I'm not worried. But my cousin? Well, she prefers things being a little more comfortable, new, and to have gates. Which is pretty funny, all in all, considering the fact that she grew up doing without, roughing it, and just getting by. Maybe that's the reason why she prefers to draw the line now, to not go back there. Maybe she just wants to make up for all the comforts she didn't have as a small child.

We pull up at our four-star. There are bars on the doors and windows. The empty lot next door is filled with rubble from a recent building demolition. The driver stops the van, and gets out and opens our door as my cousin studies the brochure and says, "This can't be right."

It is. We enter the gates and wait for the desk clerk. Our room is right behind the breakfast nook, which is right behind the desk clerk's desk. It's a little less than what my cousin was expecting. She keeps saying, "Are you sure this is right?" as we are given a huge key to lock our door at night.

"This place really is old," I tell her. "See, it says historic."

"This just isn't what I was expecting."

"I know, but it's all right." I look at the architecture, imagine what the old house used to look like, imagine how this "historic" part of the city used to be part of a thriving place to live.

"C'mon. Let's go explore, find a grocery store, get some supplies."

"Are you sure?"

"Of course, people around here eat in this neighborhood. It's okay."

As a writer, I could pour out thousands of words about this seven-day trip across the country, through the mountains and down to the coast. But what I want to say most is that I continued to pray for strangers all along the way. From the incredibly beautiful, funny, friendly people who worked at that first "four-star" hotel to those who served us dinner at a resort that was exceptional in every way—even exceeding my cousin's expectations.

One woman, a young mother with a small child, was

riding the bus to visit relatives for a holiday. The holiday had also produced numerous wrecks on the roads between here and there, causing us to take multiple side trips, cutting through muddy trails where the van almost didn't make it. Our two-and-a-half-hour ride became a seven-hour journey during which I was able to speak in broken Spanish, the woman in broken English, as we tried to tell our stories to one another through the rough ride while the baby clambered and crawled between our feet and over our knees. I tried my best to explain to her that I wished her special blessings and prayers, and hugged her before she left. And now she's out there somewhere in that country south of me carrying on, and I'm here and remembering her in this moment. Remembering her and a host of other people, the driver that night who delivered us once again to our "historic" hotel so late into the evening that the gates were closed up tight. We couldn't get in and would have been left in the dark on the sidewalk in a really bad part of town. We eventually woke up the desk clerk, but this driver refused to leave us, even offering to bring us to his home so his wife could cook us a late-night meal and we'd have a safe place to sleep.

Then there was the young guide who took us on the skywalk through the rain forest, the hotel clerk who gave me such a great history lesson of the entire country as I sat entranced with the story, the waitresses, and schoolchildren. Since the trip happened on my birthday, my cousin was determined that in some way it be memorable. Being in Costa Rica was plenty. I can spend birthdays quietly reflecting, celebrating in my own sweet way, simply being grateful for one more year, for family, friends, and love. My cousin—not so much. She is determined that my birthday must contain fanfare of some sort, and she is determined that I have lunch at the lodge where we are now staying in the rain forest region.

Okay, so we are having lunch. There are only two other tables in the entire place. The waitresses approach the table with a birthday cake and put it before me, smiling, then they begin to sing "Happy Birthday" in Spanish. I'm so very much wishing my cousin had not put me through this as the five-year-old kid in me surfaces once again and wants to leave the room. Then I look down at the cake. That's when I begin to cry. Someone has taken more time and trouble to decorate this cake than is feasible. Flower petals are arranged just so, fresh-picked flower blossoms circling the entire cake. The waitress hugs me and says, "You are sad? Don't be sad. Be happy. It's your birthday." I wipe away tears, trying to explain that they are happy tears but happy really isn't what I mean. They are grateful tears. Appreciative tears. I ask to go to the kitchen, where I find this little woman working.

"*Gracias, gracias,*" I tell her as I give her a hug. "*Bueno, bueno.*"

Then I try to use a lot of other words, to get the waitress to communicate for me about prayers and blessings and strangers. About goodness and how it transcends borders and places, about how eternal the human heart really is. I must learn other languages so that I can communicate this; for some reason, it is vitally important to me.

Then my cousin says, "Man, I didn't know you were going to take it like that. I was just trying to get you a cake, you know?"

"Yeah, I know. C'mon, let's call one of those rocky road cabs to take us into the city."

So we go out to celebrate on a rainy day, in a town of a few hundred people. We walk the streets, watch the clouds move over the mountains, find a place for a glass of wine and a toast to happy birthdays, and to the people of Costa Rica. I say a prayer for them, one and all.

TO TELL OR NOT TO TELL

**You can pray for someone even if
you don't think God exists.**

—REAL LIVE PREACHER

IT WAS ONE OF THOSE DAYS AGAIN. FOR WHAT FELT LIKE THE three-hundredth time, I decided I just wasn't going to tell anyone that I was praying for them. It goes against my nature. It takes courage. It takes time; all those blessed interferences take me away from other obligations and pursuits. It takes some kind of faith to believe that my prayers might matter to a stranger. The bottom line—it takes.

But it also gives.

But today I'm thinking this act of telling just takes too much. I'll continue to say my prayers, but I'll just keep it to myself. In spite of all the positive reinforcement I've received over the year, in spite of the gratitude and the days when I seemingly shifted the world for someone in the direction of hope or light—I still want to keep to myself, put my nose in a book, and study prayer more than pray for the multitudes one person at a time.

Yes, studying seems a great and worthy endeavor. I could study those desert fathers again, the solitary praying mothers, the saints of old and new. I could study how the Buddhists pray or the Jesuit priests, I could study everything and anything about the act of praying without getting my spiritual hands dirty, rolling up my sleeves, and getting into this messy melee.

After all, it would be meaningful research with historical references. I'm getting excited the more I think about it. Images of me poring over volumes of spiritual notes and letters, the late afternoon sun casting its light through the dusty air, bathing me in a holy glow. I would study diligently, make great outlines, and fill them in with poetic prose that pointed to the spiritual truths and experiences of thousands.

Then an old man walks past me, and before I can even clear those glorified daydreams from my mind, I reach out and touch his shoulder saying, "Look here, here's the thing." My storytelling mouth gets ahead of my mind again. "I pray for someone really special that crosses my path every day. Today you are that person."

There is the slightest of shifts in the air. I feel it, and recognize it for that welcoming gratefulness that it is. When someone takes a deep breath that almost equals an Amen. I check the name tag he's wearing and say, "Robert, man, I just want you to know that all day long and into the night I'm going to be thinking about you."

He nods his head real slow. A movement that says, *Yes, yes.* He turns to go, saying, "Oh, I sure do need that. I surely do."

"We all do, honey. We all sure do," I say. Then we both go our separate ways, both of us commiserating in the spirit on how much we sure do need prayer.

So much for my romantic image of research in the book stacks. To tell or not to tell? I never know for certain and fight the urge every step of the way. But when I think about all the Roberts I've met, and the people like him for whom, for some reason, a few words from this stranger girl seems to be good medicine, then I agree with Robert. We sure do need it. It looks like my days of hiding in the books are over.

I believe we greatly underestimate our power to pray, to affect someone's story in a positive way. For that one word, one touch to be something that they carry home with them and hold steady in their hearts.

Shut In but Not Out

The feeling remains that God is on the journey, too.

—SAINT TERESA OF AVILA

I'VE WRITTEN A LOT AND TOLD A NUMBER OF STORIES ABOUT the people who have crossed my path. I've stopped people outside elevators, tapped them in parking lots, spoken to them in doctors' offices, met them in grocery stores. As I look back at the past year, there are a trail of people that I've prayed for. Some I've told and some I've just kept that business to myself. More often than not, when I didn't tell, nine times out of ten I wished later that I would have. It's just what works for me, what I feel led to do, but for others that might not be the case at all. I think the act of praying is huge, the act of consideration of another human being and their life—a moment to wonder what they are going through and to care—is paramount. The telling is something strange and wonderful but not something required.

But I do think when people are praying for me that it

makes a difference in my life. I know praying for others certainly does. That's why I've continued to do so on days when I was alone or busy. Even days when I never left home. There are still thousands of people at my doorstep needing a special whisper of blessing.

There have been days that I prayed for people in the news, a face from the newspaper, a person on Facebook, or from the profile of a person on Twitter. In these days of social media and massive social interaction through the Internet, there's no end to the number of people that I can touch in a positive way without ever stepping foot outside my door. The beautiful thing is it still counts.

A beautiful friend of mine has embraced this idea of praying for a stranger. She's retired and not able to drive anymore. Much of her life is spent at home. Regardless of the fact that she is less mobile, there are no boundaries or borders that stop her from praying, from offering something good and wonderful for a stranger each day.

I want to bottle her enthusiasm. I want to keep and remember what started as a resolution for me hasn't ended that way. And my many days of "having to" has become the blessing of "wanting to." There are really no restrictions and no end to the possibilities.

INCONVENIENT LOVE

**Our prayer must not be self-centered. It must
arise not only because we feel our own need as a
burden we must lay upon God, but also because we
are so bound up in love for our fellow men that we feel
their need as acutely as our own. To make intercession
for men is the most powerful and practical way in
which we can express our love for them.**

—JOHN CALVIN

THEY SEEMED TO BE A LONELY COUPLE. NOT IN THEIR togetherness, but isolated in some way from the other dining room patrons. For one, he was visibly impaired. Something, an old injury, an illness perhaps, was keeping him from really eating or making conversation. They sat a few tables away from us. Occasionally, I made eye contact with the woman, and it was one of those stranger moments where that connection is a shade deeper than just catching someone's eye on the street.

We order Thai food, Thai beer, and just really try to recover from our day, but the man and woman are somehow present with us. I hear a waiter saying dessert is included in their meal. I know this place well; know the menu like the back of my hand. Dessert isn't included in anything. When they get ready to leave, I have that crazy, stranger feeling. I want to tell them but don't want to bring attention to the man's condition. I don't want to single him out for this, to make him feel I was feeling oh-so-sorry for him.

We nod our good-byes as they leave the restaurant. Later, after we've lingered over dinner, after we have discussed the people who were almost our tablemates, brought up praying for strangers and what that's like on a daily basis, my husband and I leave. We've come in separate vehicles, arriving from different places. Now, it's late, we're tired, it's time to go home. I pull out of the parking lot behind him onto the four-lane highway, and as I do, I look to my right to discover the couple from the restaurant sitting at a bus stop in the dark. I'm almost to the red light when my phone rings.

"I know," I say. It's my husband, who saw them also.

"Are the buses even running this late?" he asks me.

"Don't think so." Then there is a pause as we both consider the implications, the complications, the nuisance of being tired and feeling at the same time a need to get involved.

"I'm turning around," I tell him. "I'll call you back."

When I pull up at the bus stop, I ask them, "Guys, are you waiting on a bus because I don't think they run this late."

"We don't know what to do. We're needing to get to a hotel for the night but that one"—she motions to a Days Inn—"is full."

I consider them and their circumstances. "Look, I've got my dog with me, but he won't bite. If you don't mind riding along, I'll take you down the road to another hotel."

"Okay, thank you." Then they start to rise, her helping the man, who rises slowly—very slowly—from the bench. Then they see my big white dog sticking his head out the window. "Never mind," they say. "He's just too big."

Well, he's not a Chihuahua, that's for sure. Understatement because he's a Great Pyrenees, and I guess when you're not used to him, he seems larger than life, possibly even deadly. There's no point in telling them he hides behind me if he hears thunder and thinks he's a lapdog.

"Would you mind just driving down and seeing if they have a room by the interstate? If you tell us they do, we'll walk down there."

"Okay," I say. And three hotels, three night desk clerks later, I'm still checking on prices and availability. My husband calls. "They won't get in the jeep with me because of Titan. He scares them." If it's possible, he's more tired than I am. "I'm turning around," he says, which is one of the reasons I love him. He was almost home but says, "I saw that man. He can't walk to the bus stop much less miles down the road," and turns back to get them.

There are times I get to simply tell someone I'm praying for them and then go on about my business. Then there are times that it's more about doing something. This time it was about turning around, getting involved in spite of the way I felt. It was about, if not embracing the compilation and inconvenience, at least not ruling it out as a possibility.

I find a hotel with a room; my husband picks up the couple even though it takes a long time to get the man in the truck because of his condition. We meet in the lobby and wait to be certain they get checked in, contribute a few dollars to the room for the night, and I try to shake the man's hand even though he can't shake hands. I reach out and squeeze his fingers. "Take care of that big dog now," he says.

Then his wife, Gloria, looks at me and says, "God bless you and thank you again." And she gives me a long hug and then holds my gaze when she releases me. She doesn't want to let me go. She wants to tell me things, to share her story, I know she does. But it's late, I'm tired, and my husband is waiting for me just beyond the sliding doors.

"Take care, Miss Gloria," I say. I call the hotel on the way home to make certain that they did indeed get checked in and make it to a room. And with doing all of that, I felt like I could have done something more. I could have—called the next morning to see if they needed a ride and then— what? Sent a cab since I was due at the radio station? Tried to discover if they had enough money to get back to Memphis, where they were headed? Encouraged them to call a friend or family member to somehow come get them or get a few dollars to them by Western Union so they could get those tickets? I'm not certain of those things or if my Good Samaritan box was sufficiently checked the night before. What I did was to pray for them, and part of that prayer was that another stranger would come along, and then another, and yet another if that's what it took to get them where they needed to go. I prayed that a chain reaction of strangers helping would make the difference. Maybe not one of us can be the end-all, do-all. Maybe the circumstances of our own lives don't allow that. But if one stranger's prayerful actions could be linked like the passing of a baton in a relay race to another's, there's hope that so many situations and conditions could be improved upon. There is hope.

EDWARD

**No one who has had a unique experience with
prayer has a right to withhold it from others.**

—SOONG MEI-LING

W HAT I AM LEARNING ON THE JOURNEY OF THIS RESOLU-
tion is not so much how my prayers might hold
power or change the course of events—what I am learning is how it is changing me. This introverted, mental,
writer girl who wants to turn to people in a buffet line
and declare, "Stop following me!" is beginning to look at
all of humanity with an open and expectant heart. Who
are these human beings from every walk of life and corner
of our society, our country, and the entire planet—who
are sharing this time on earth with me? Some may be on
their way in, as brand-new as one-minute breath, and others barely moving to the beat of a drummer three generations old, but our times on the surface of this earth have
overlapped. Here we are together. All of us. And then the

woman behind me in the buffet line isn't quite cramming my space, or the cabdriver, or the doctor. We are souls here on this planet full of dreams and heartaches and big love. Yet in so many ways we move through not touching one another, not connecting.

This experience of walking out this resolution is showing me something completely opposite. That in spite of what we might think in our isolated worlds, dens, neighborhoods, we are connected in remarkable unseen ways. My prayer chart looks like a big connect-the-dots. The woman who was afraid of losing her house, the woman who had already lost hers and moved into a trailer, the old man slumped behind the wheel with heavy burdens, the girl praying for her bipolar mother, that small, abused child—we are as connected and purposed as those wild stars in the sky. Everything seems so happenstance and yet, if we study science, the way the forest works with the animals, the way the wildfires clean the forest, the connection is concrete and indisputable. When I look now at the faces I've met, the connections are evident in our common humanity. The randomness of our exchanges no longer feels that way to me but more like the exchanges we have with each other are indeed part of a greater plan.

I'm in a grocery store, and I'm rushing, needing to get home and dressed for a special literary event. So I'm in the deli, buying my husband one of his favorite sandwiches for dinner. I order and stand at the counter, waiting and look-

ing around the store in the process, but I feel eyes on me. It's
a universal kind of human awareness, isn't it, when we are
being watched? I am, and there he is. This man watching is
sitting in the little deli with a pencil in his hand and a note-
pad in front of him. He has bright red hair, and a red beard. A
little tired looking but smiling at me, and something about
him strikes me as—what? Very otherworldly. That's the only
way to say it. I smile and turn back around, trying to concentrate on my husband's sandwich in the making, but that
familiar nudge is there. This is where I begin my internal dialogue again, that I don't have time to talk to a stranger, that
I'm already running late as usual. I never get over this part.
But the difference about this man hangs tangibly in my mind.
Picture a *Lord of the Rings* character out of time and place, off
the movie set, and sitting right there in the grocery deli and
you'll understand. So I think, *I'll pray for him but I don't have to tell
him.* Then I turn and walk over to the table in the deli.

If I'd told you the opening I gave everyone, it would
bore you to tears. It's always about the same—"What's your
name? . . . I have this thing I do every day . . . This year my
resolution . . . Today you're my stranger." That part may be
routine, but the praying for people is not. The people are
not ever the same.

"Edward's my name," he says.

I tell him that I'll be praying for him and for him to
receive special blessings, for his needs to be met whatever
they may be.

"You have no idea how much I needed to hear that," he says and begins to write something in his notebook. I start to walk away, but I'm moved to explain something to him. I go back and stand before his table.

"Listen," I tell him. "You have no idea what doing this has meant to *me*. This year I have two sons deployed. One in Iraq, one in Afghanistan. I think this resolution has somehow been saving my life." He smiles as I continue. "Every day it forces me to walk through the world with my eyes open, to see other people's needs, and not just concentrate on my own fears. I could have just caved in on myself in a state of all that I need, praying for my own, you know. Really, this prayer stuff for everyone else, it's as much for me as it is for you. I just wanted you to know." And then I start to walk away again and he calls for me. When I turn back, he looks me in the eye and says, "You listen to me now." He holds up a finger for emphasis. "Your sons are going to be all right. They'll be coming home and they're gonna make it."

Here he is, this little red-haired man, with his little notebook he's been writing in, and that otherworldly look in his eye.

"You know something?" I tell him. "I believe you."

There are moments in life where we follow the leading of our spirits. I knew from the moment I saw him that in a world where other dimensions exist and beings might just cross over on occasion, perhaps he was an angel watching and on assignment. Just think of a benevolent, slightly shabby, rumpled *It's a Wonderful Life* kind of an angel. Or maybe just a very ordinary rumpled, redheaded man who has an amazingly good message. Either way, it's fine with me.

Last Words

Look at everything as though you were seeing
it for the first time or the last time. Then your
time on earth will be filled with glory.

—BETTY SMITH

I'VE BEEN THINKING LATELY ABOUT LAST WORDS. ABOUT THE
way we pass strangers all day, passing words back and
forth of common courtesy or general irritation. I've been
thinking about how any of these words could be our last.
Then, of course, I consider husbands and wives and mothers and fathers and friends, the people in our lives that we
live with every day, still not saying the things that matter so
much, still being courteous or irritated.

So here I was thinking about final words. The last chance
we have to leave an imprint on a person's heart. What is the
perfect phrasing that says it all?

Then I heard them. The *perfect last words*. They were graced
upon me by my friend the last time I ever saw him alive. And

before I knew it, a few days later, he was in a coma and then he was gone. A victim of what one relative has called *"that old disease they don't have no cure for."* Funny thing was, I knew he had taken a turn for the worse but I wasn't expecting his leaving. Not that soon. I might have said some things. Some *different* things. But I think about his words to me and the way that he *delivered* them. He cut through to the chase. He dropped the pretense and pleasantries that exist between even the closest of friends. He didn't even talk about *himself*, which in healthier times he did—*a lot.* (This was one of the things that we joked about.) But he was a visionary and an artist and a talented man. He had a lot to say, a lot he wanted to share. But in the end, he had only one thing. The words he left behind. The final ones that he bestowed upon those who dared to draw near.

Again and again, as years go by, I turn those words over like precious stones; bring them to the surface of my mind. He said them with an honesty that only comes when that sheet of time hanging between mortal and immortal fades into the light. "I love you *so* much," he said. You would have to have heard him to know how much he meant those words. How much he felt them. How much I feel them still.

Now, I find myself praying for strangers everywhere. Speaking to them during the day, remembering them in the night, and I'm wondering what if those words, those few words spoken, were my final here on earth or maybe the last that they received. What if this stranger, this one right here in front of me today, is one of the most important people in my life, or that I'm the last living contact they'll receive? I'm not being morbid, just factually curious. It happens. Our final chance meetings. If that's the case, perhaps leaning forward, pausing just a moment and whispering to someone, *Today you are my special stranger I'm praying blessings for*—is not such a long, horrible, frightful step to make.

May all our final words, to friends and foes, to strangers one and all, be so divine.

THE SECRET OF PRAYER

Prayer is more than meditation. In meditation the source of strength is one's self. When one prays he goes to a source of strength greater than his own.

—CHIANG KAI-SHEK

WHAT EXACTLY IS THIS POWER, THIS THING WE CALL prayer?

Tonight I think of all the praying that's taking place in quiet rooms and behind closed doors. Of old, worn knees kneeling on cold floors. Of prayers being said in many nations for children, for the cares and concerns of this world, for old dogs and new dreams. Prayers whispered all through the night everywhere. What am I doing this year? How bizarre to yoke myself to something so invisibly tangible.

I don't even know how to write this book. Truth. Cross my heart and bare my soul. I'm a fiction writer primarily. This is not fiction. The stories in this book are true although when I come home and tell my husband the latest stranger interaction, he says, "No one will believe these things happened." He is wrong. The people that I've talked to in airports, restaurants, and neighborhoods across many states know they are true.

Now today I'm wondering, as the world is getting colder outside on this late October evening, what if we all did this silly little thing like pray for a stranger every day. Could the world be shaped by our good thoughts for one another? Could it be made whole or better? I ask you to try. I know that's personal but I mean it. It doesn't have to be your resolution, or your everyday discipline. I simply ask you to be aware of the multitudes—one person at a time. As you move through your daily life, as you flip the channel on TV, Facebook another friend, you are brushing up against souls full of worry. People in despair. People who have their heads down because they are crying and don't want you to see. How raw and exposed we feel when someone sees us hurting, but after almost a year of this insane endeavor, I've come to realize that, on any given day, we are all hurting in one way or another.

Again, I don't know why people pray. I only know why I do. Just this morning one of my good friends and fellow writers is facing some serious health risks and challenges. I thought about her and kinda prayed. By that I mean that I prayed something like—*Dear God, make Sally well.* And then I thought about her some more. Then I really prayed.

Sometimes I can feel my heart in my prayers, sometimes my mind, and other times, actually a shifting kind of power. As if my prayers hold weight and water. When this happens, I feel as if I've made a difference in the natural world somehow.

So this book in some ways is about me praying and about whether any of it really matters. I'm here to tell you that it matters. No matter what has gone wrong, no matter how any of your prayers have not been answered, it still matters. You and me praying for others, for each other, matters.

Sometimes I think I will stop this nonsense. Or this habit, or this resolution. Whatever you want to call it, I will not quit now. This practice keeps my awareness of people around me turned up so much higher. On many days I just want that light shut down. I want to move through the waters of my day anonymous and unseen. Then a feverish baby looks up at me from a grocery cart and I freeze frame that face instantly and know that baby is my stranger for the day. I just say a prayer for that baby, for his life, for his destiny. And the weirdest thing of all to me is how that face will be locked into my memory because here's the thing about me—I'm a loser. Meaning I lose things—papers, keys, glasses, names—I lose a name the moment it's uttered. Even when I think I will remember it, five minutes after I leave that person, it's gone—that is, unless I write it down with notes of explanation: Chicago, book club, restaurant, this person ate the blue cheese chicken and told a joke about feathers.

This year, faces are never lost, not forgotten. It's as if my spirit takes a snapshot, and while their names may fade unless I write them in my journal, their faces never do. Not the babies, not the old people, not the people I tell or don't tell. And I have my reasons. Sometimes telling would embarrass them. Sometimes they are so down and out that they'd feel I was—even worse—taking pity on them, and that's never the case.

Let me get this straight also—I don't know what I'm doing. This is not a science and I'm not special. I'm just trying my best to fulfill a resolution.

Imprint

You can't stay in your corner of the Forest
waiting for others to come to you.
You have to go to them sometimes.

—WINNIE THE POOH

I CAN SEE THAT THIS IS HOW IT'S GOING TO BE NOW. I'LL BE AN old, old woman living out my last days, watching the birds eat, taking the time to concentrate on the colors at their throats and hidden in their wings, and then it will happen. There will be a flash of a face from thirty-odd years ago. A moment of passing and connecting between two strangers. I have a myriad of faces tattooed on my spirit. In quiet moments they appear unsummoned. A woman from a hotel lobby, a waitress from a diner, a man in a garage, their faces, their requests, their hearts' desires, rising and floating within me like the tides. Somehow I've been integrated into the human race in a new way.

I had thought that little by little the faces would fade

away over the days and months gone by, that they would sink below some memory waterline, never to be thought of again. I was wrong. I thought it was a nice little resolution for a year, something to put on like a coat and shed like an old skin at the ringing in of the new year. That's not the way it's going to be. It's becoming a lifestyle, this awareness, this otherness.

I used to search diligently for just one face, one person that stood out to me. And while I still do that, I'm also aware of what's going on around me throughout the day and what struck me as true so very long ago stands out to me even more today: The world needs prayer. More appropriately, it needs more people praying from a place of compassionate concern.

Could it stand to reason that a man or woman, that even a child, could propel a people or a good purpose forward? Does one person praying for one person they pass really matter? A hundred people praying? A million? Would we all be imprinted with these memories of strangers' faces, of funny little moments and occurrences where we made a human connection that for some bizarre reason continues to last beyond any logical reasons why?

When a plane goes down on its way to Paris with no survivors, that's no longer a thirty-second sound bite on the news at five for me. It's a plane full of strangers with family and friends who were waiting on them at the airport. When the rolls of the dead are called out from tragedies of all kinds, I consider their life stories and what they were like. I don't mean this in a morbid, worrisome kind of way. But if this year has shown me anything, it is that we are not alone. We traveled here together, and we'll all be leaving the same way with a few minor details to separate us. This time, this moment that we are passing in the streets, the diners, the trains—they are somehow so perfect in their hope and their possibilities for us to be better to one another. One person, one stranger, one prayer at a time.

TRUTH AND MYSTERY

God does not stand afar off as I struggle to speak.
He cares enough to listen with more than casual
attention. He translates my scrubby words and
hears what is truly inside. He hears my sighs
and uncertain gropings as fine prose.

—TIMOTHY JONES

THERE ARE MANY REASONS I DIDN'T WANT TO WRITE THIS book. The only one that matters, the one I come back to, is for all my public life, writer-girl business, all my laughing and joking around on stage, or cutting up with friends, I am one of the most private people you'll ever meet. My closest friends understand this. My husband still doesn't get it sometimes when I don't want him to share certain details or stories with friends. *Who cares?* he'll say. Me. The funny stories I tell are usually about things that happened along the way or family stories. And the most personal, private part of my life, forever and ever and truly, is my private relationship with God and my prayer life. And here I am baring my soul on paper and revealing what I consider the most intimate part of my creation.

I once took a philosophy course in college with an amazing professor. We were assigned to keep journals of our lives and include some pretty personal things but always in the light of having an analytical mind for self-evaluation and integrating the things we had learned in the process. I got an A+ on my first journal. Then the next grading period came out and I think I received an A- with a note written across the top that asked, *Where is God?*

Excuse me? I was appalled. I had to make an appointment to go speak with the professor. "God," I told him, "was private." I'd rather talk about my sex life if I had to. God was something so personal that I wouldn't dare to include that kind of intimacy or to ever psychoanalyze, break down, and discuss anything about how God fit into my life!

So now here I am writing this book that started out as just a quiet resolution. Just something between me and God, and oh, you know, the rest of the world. But something began to happen along the way. For one thing, the stories were coming and I kept shoving them in my pocket just to pull out and tell my husband later. But he kept asking——"Are you writing these down? You have to be writing these down."

Like most good writers, sometimes I'm diligent and sometimes I'm not. Sometimes I write, but sometimes I am tired and I put it off until the next day. But the stories kept coming. And some of those are included here as examples, I suppose, of what's going on out there in the world.

I like visiting God on his terms and my terms as long as the two collide nicely. This resolution business has been messy. It has required me to think and to be aware of other people on a master scale of things. Let me get something straight between us—if God's plan for salvation for mankind was to stick me on a street corner and ask people if they knew God, then we would all be in trouble. I'd be like, "Nice dog you have there. And is that Lyle Lovett you're listening to on that iPod? Read any good books lately? Sure is a pretty day, isn't it?" I don't think God would come up at all. Not on my account. And not even in a general, ethereal kind of way. But ultimately, when all is said and done, I'm a purveyor of hidden truth, of the mystery and the divine. And I'm a storyteller. So if you said to me, *River, tell me a God story,* I'd pull up a chair and begin at the beginning. That's what I've tried to do here.

The storyteller in me is more than a little amazed and overwhelmed by the stories that have been offered to me. Of the simple ways that I've been invited to be a part of someone else's story. It has been a humbling experience. Instead of discovering how much the world needs me, I've discovered that I was the one who needed the world.

I believe words have destinies, like people, and these have found their way into your hands for good reason. So here I go, baring my soul and telling the truth. And it's not even for a grade.

My truth, my faith, has evolved and matured in a variety of ways. I've had a few strange occurrences along the way. But not lost on me is, in looking back over my life, that I have been praying for a long time for one thing or another, even as a small child gazing out my window into the night sky with something like silent prayers on my lips. I think they were just prayers of wonder about the stars.

I get the following question from time to time. "So, tell me"—eyelashes lowered over a glass of wine—"just how religious are you?"

"Not very," I say. And that's the truth. Me and religion don't cozy. Me and the mystery? Well, that's a different story.

Sometimes I remind myself of that character Sidney Poitier played in *Lilies of the Field*. The Mother Superior declares in a heavy German accent, "God has sent me a big, strong man . . . to build a chapel [pronounced 'shapel']!" To which Sidney's character replies, "I don't know 'bout no chapel."

I'm just your everyday, slightly culturally enlightened, introverted writer. I'm a product, to a huge degree, of my generation. Most days I don't know nothin' 'bout no shapel either. I'm just walking out my journey one day at a time like everyone else. But what I am learning when I pray for strangers is that I fully expect those prayers to be answered for the simple reason that this act is carried out from one soul to another without any personal agenda attached. The faith attached to those prayers is tangible, sometimes more than others. When I pray for those closest to me, all those prayers are a part of my selfish heart. Yes, I pray out of love for them but also for my need for that love to continue. For them to be well, happy, successful. For them to thrive in their lives that I might find happiness.

I'm beginning to see that the part of me that reaches out to the homeless and the well-to-do, the young and the aged, the broken and lost, is the one that matters most. My heart has opened up so much further than I ever dreamed possible. These strangers, this adventure, are making me a better person in spite of myself. Once an internal recluse, I'm more open to not only meeting people, but opening myself up to truly caring what happens in their lives. I'm more patient to listen on my better days. And it must be obvious in some way. They find me on the streets, in libraries, and on street corners. They even find me in my dreams. Just last night, a face I would have thought long forgotten was suddenly there speaking her soft, simple requests. A small reminder of her existence. When I awoke, I lay there a minute pulling her from my sleep and days past to the present moment. And I said another prayer for her, one more hopeful blessing for a soul I had encountered many, many months ago.

That's the way it is now: These people and their stories are no longer shadowy extras, character walk-ons cruising the periphery of my life. Their stories have become integrated into the fabric of my own. Perhaps the poets and prophets were right all along. We don't come into this world separate, or belonging to a select few, but we're a part of the human race. All of us amazingly the same in spite of our differences. This is the real thing. We belong to each other. We always have. And in the process of my understanding this, of walking out this resolution, I've lost my regret and instead have counted it lost if I don't touch a life, offer a smile, a prayer, a pause along the way. So every day I continue to do this one tiny thing. This one tiny, incredible thing.

What readers are saying about
PRAYING *for* STRANGERS

My name is Maura. I am writing you a short note before I have even finished *Praying for Strangers*, with a profound thank-you. I have cried; I have laughed; I have delighted. I have felt the blessing of having it reaffirmed in such beautiful ways that ALL moments of connection matter. That prayer matters. I have always been deeply touched by the chance encounters and stories and prayers that ensued as I paused to hold a door a little longer or found myself with the time to hear or see and talk with those I met throughout my day.

I'm always amazed at the depth that transpires in a brief few minutes when we just take the time to look someone in the eyes, acknowledge their presence, their gift of being, saying hello and giving a blessing. Coming from New York, where eye contact was to the ground, this has been a slow, beautiful evolution to open to those around me.

Some days I am more open than others. My most recent unexpected gift was the biggest bear hug coming towards me, gruff whiskers and a whiff of alcohol, from an elated homeless man exclaiming, "Open my heart to see." Years ago I would have backed or run away, but in this one unexpected moment of exchange I went for the connection. Although it had that slow, "Okay, God, here we go" feel to it as I opened my heart to the unexpected. I was left smiling, knowing that it came from some divine intervention for both of us.

This last Christmas my husband and I—for the first time ever—sent a book that came into our path to a long list of people that spoke to us on a deep level . . . both the people and the book. As I have read *Praying for Strangers*, a new list has evolved in my head of people who would be deeply touched by the gift of your book. My list of names grows by the chapters. I ordered my first extra copies, which I am hand delivering this week, and from there the order will grow and go out until I run out of names. So part of what I want to say is "You are my author." The one I have chosen to send forth into the small world, knowing that your words will touch and transform how we see each other.

River, blessings and prayers of thanksgiving for you and your beautiful book. It is so delightfully honest and human.

I have only written a few authors in my lifetime who have

profoundly touched me and made a difference. Unlike the others, for you I didn't even wait to finish the book or wait for the perfectly edited, polished, best-things-to-say letter . . . I just wanted to say thank-you in whatever raw form it came right in the middle of it all. It is a gift your words have come into my life at this time. Thank you for the gift of you making your way in this beautiful, imperfect world, discovering and celebrating our connectedness!

Abundant blessings and peace.

—Maura Walsh

My name is JerriLyn. I'm fifty years old and I live in a suburb of Portland, Oregon, with my husband and sons. I just finished your book *Praying for Strangers* and just want you to know that it has had such a great impact on my life.

I was roaming through Powell's bookstore in Beaverton one day and your book caught my eye. I'm not a big reader; in fact, I feel I must make a confession at this point, since I never knew of you or your writings previously (please forgive me for this delay). Anyway, I stopped, started to read the cover, then a few pages. It was very intriguing to me and I was excited to see that some of the copies had been autographed. I decided to buy a few copies. One for myself and some others for friends, etc. Let me tell you, this was the best decision I had ever made!

I became a believer at a young age and would find myself

feeling an urge, a prompting to pray for people I didn't know. If a plane flew overhead, I would pray for the person sitting in a certain seat . . . row D, seat two . . . that kind of thing . . . just praying that they would have a good day, that they would know that Jesus loved them, and so on. I would do this when I heard a siren or saw an ambulance passing by—pray for the person hurt or for the policeman that was responding. I have done this all along but of course was not brave enough to tell the "stranger" I had just prayed for them. What an amazing thing! I haven't made it a daily occurrence nor have I gone up to the stranger to let them know what I have done, but I'm getting closer to taking the big step! You have shown me and others that there is nothing to lose but everything to gain . . . so I will do it!

The one thing I realize about praying for others is that it helps me to stop dwelling on myself and on my circumstances. I've really needed to look outward and upward instead of inward.

I have pretty much bought out your book from Powell's bookstore and have given copies to others who would be blessed to read it as well. I'm hoping to give out more copies to more people so they, too, can have an awakening in their spirit as I have had.

Thanks again for taking the time to not only pray for strangers but to let us be a part of the journey with you.

Take care and I will remember to pray for you, too!

—JerriLyn Korth

I just started your book tonight and read only through the second chapter, "Blue Shoes," and the power that it has led me to this e-mail to say so.

But even before I opened the book, the title led me to the same starting line you encountered to pray for strangers. The title itself had the power to move me, as a believer, to pray for not just loved ones but all those who cross my path.

The power of prayer is a wonderful free gift that we need to constantly be aware of, and your book is just what I need in "this season."

Thank you again for your wisdom, and tomorrow I am anxious to read a few more chapters.

—John J. Zapatka, Jr.

Can't tell you how much I love *Praying for Strangers* . . . My husband and I have both finished it and it truly has changed our lives . . . Taking my copy to my pastor this week and know he will love it, too . . . I know I am gushing, but it is very sincere! We have what we call "River Jordan" moments all the time now! In Walmart a few weeks ago, my husband was an aisle away and he called out, "Hey, babe," looking for me—a woman working there answered because she thought he said, "Hey, ma'am." We got a good laugh out of it, and then she told us she hasn't been called *babe* in seven years, since her husband died . . . We talked for a few minutes and I have been praying for her and see her face in my mind every day since . . .

—Melissa Jaggers

~

The night that I came to see you at FoxTale in Atlanta and you shared *Praying for Strangers*, I knew that God wanted me to do this! I was so touched by your caring spirit and I knew that I wanted to be a part of this wonderful spiritual journey. So I started praying for people immediately. It's funny because when you are cognizant of praying for someone, the person just seems to come to you. People ask me how I determine who I am going to pray for that day and how in the world I tell them that I'm going to pray for them, but it is really so easy.

I have prayed for people in the grocery store that I pass by or I'm in line with, people who work at the post office, a lady who asked my husband for help with getting her gas cover off, and on and on. I just introduce myself and tell them that I choose at least one stranger to pray for each day. I ask their name and if they have anything in particular that they would like me to pray for. I have NEVER been met with anything but kindness, surprise, a sense from them that they feel special, and gratefulness on their part. Most ask for prayers for themselves and for their families. They usually deal with health and well-being. So far no one has asked for me to pray that they win the lottery or that they get a new car or house. People seem genuinely amazed that someone cares enough to think about them throughout the day in the effort to make their life better. They have all been appreciative and everyone has thanked me for praying for them. What they don't realize is that I should be thanking them because I, too, am receiving great blessings from this special time that I spend with God. I know that this may sound funny, but I have noticed that people smile at me a lot more since I have begun doing this. I believe that praying for others does more for me than anyone else because it makes me feel closer to God and like I am doing something to help someone else. I plan to keep doing this for as long as I am able, and know that your idea and your book will make fantastic positive change in the lives of so many people around the world. And I'm especially glad that I have the opportunity to be one of them.

—Anita Buice

I have never written to an author regarding a book I've read, but what makes this so interesting to me is I have just read three chapters. Waking up on this beautiful Saturday morning at six thirty, I find myself opening your book and within the first few pages I'm feeling overwhelmed by my emotions. I keep reading but I find myself putting the book down to close my eyes and cry. It hits me in the pit of my stomach, so I know that "praying for strangers" is a concept I can internalize and allow under my skin. So much of how you describe yourself feels somehow familiar to me. I have so many good—great—

intentions and then I get swept off to my own world. When I was little, everyone would say, "She's going to be a preacher someday." Well, that never interested me. I still can't see myself preaching anything, but I can pray for strangers.

Thank you for writing this book.

—Rindy Leeds

I was so captivated by [your book] it was hard to put it down. I finished reading it in just a few days. I was inspired . . . and feel like everyone could learn a little from this book. I know it took a lot of gumption for you to keep up this resolution when sometimes it would have been easier to say, "No, not today." I talked to my daughter about how inspired I was about this book, so she suggested, "Why don't we do this for Lent?" and I agreed although it will be much tougher on her than on me. I'll talk to anyone. But my daughter is more like you and is introverted by nature. She does not like to be around a lot of people and does not approach people unless she has to. So on Ash Wednesday we will start our Lenten resolution to pray for a stranger every day and pick them at random as you did in the book. Thank you so much for taking on this resolution and writing this memoir that is so inspirational. I look forward to sharing it with friends. My daughter is reading it now and loving every word of it. It doesn't seem that "thank you" is enough.

—Mary Yetta Alexander

I never write to authors, but I must tell you that I was deeply touched by this book. I recently told my husband, "I can't read this book anymore before work. The tears are ruining my makeup!" I was terribly serious. I'm reading it at night now—after makeup removal. Ha!

Thank you for sharing your resolution with us. I, too, am now praying for strangers. I shared your book and resolution with my little Bible group at work and now several of them are praying for strangers, too.

—Kathy Green

I am not the type of person who would be compelled to read a book with the word *praying* in the title, but I ABSOLUTELY LOVE THIS BOOK! I am typically a reader of fiction, but I was given a copy of *Praying for Strangers* and began reading it with no idea of what to expect. The words grabbed me and held me. The book moved me to think about humanity in a different way. I am a better person for having read this book. I just ordered twelve copies to give to the important people in my life!

—Ellen Highberger Hicks

Am halfway through *Praying for Strangers*. It. Is. Amazing. Unbelievably amazing. You, in your honesty, simplicity, and gorgeous prose, have gone straight to the heart—to my heart and soul. This is a beautiful soul-sharing, and I am thrilled with the book, with your writing, and with what this book means to me and will to so many people. Just had to let you know.

—Karen Schwettman

I am almost finished with your book *Praying for Strangers*. This book has inspired me like no other book I have ever read except the Bible! I was diagnosed with breast cancer last year and have received huge amounts of prayer. As I read your book, I was so moved that I told myself it is time to pray for others in the way you brought out in your book. So my resolution is just that, and I have already started and have received the wonderful results just like you bring out in your book.

Thank you for writing with honesty, and thank you for writing this book.

—Tammy Tallant

You may remember me from our favorite Thai restaurant in Destin, Royal Orchid. We met several months ago when you were there helping your mother-in-law and I was there working on my play. Anyway, since then you have been busy with your new book! Congratulations. It is wonderful. I was anxious to read it because you and I had met, and am glad that I did. Also, I thought you would appreciate a little story. My dear friend and former roommate from Rye, New York, called me today. She and I talk a few times a year, and we always give each other book recommendations. We are both in book clubs, so reading is a common passion. She didn't have much time to chat, but she said, "Listen, I just wanted to tell you about this great book I just read. I have already given copies to four friends, and I think you would love it, too. It is called *Praying for Strangers*, and the author is a woman named River Jordan." I said, "Cecily! I told you about her a few months ago, remember? I told you that I met her in a restaurant in Florida." Then it all started to come back to her. Anyway, I just thought you would like to hear that my friend in New York is spreading the word about your wonderful book. And she made a special call to me just to suggest it. Nice, huh?

That is all. Just wanted to share the love.

—Donna Gay Anderson

On the surface, the concept is simple. Keep your eyes and ears open, follow that inner voice, and pray for a stranger each day. Oh, but when told through the voice of a marvelous writer, it is so much more. [*Praying for Strangers*] is inspiring stuff, potentially life-changing even. The book not only entertains, it draws out laughter, tears, and a bubbling, infectious belief that we, too, can pray for strangers and be changed ourselves in the process.

—Eric Wilson

I'm having trouble reading your book because I keep crying all over the page, making it hard to read. This is the book you were always meant to write. It is moving, profound, genuine. I can't imagine anyone who would not relate to its message. Thank you for this.

—Ellen Ward

This is a necessary book. I say this because few books have ever touched me the way *Praying for Strangers* has. I've always believed in the kaleidoscope we all live in and move in. This book has given me a glimpse of how I could behave on my very best day if I were open to the world around me. This book is that heartfelt. That divine.

—Bren McClain

I was at a [bookstore] in Manhattan yesterday and my eyes fell on your book *Praying for Strangers*. I have only read about thirty pages so far, but I already know that I have found a gem. I will be recommending it to friends. I know it will have a strong positive impact on them. Thank you and congratulations on making a BIG difference.

—Ralph Powell

Readers Guide to
PRAYING *for* STRANGERS

Praying for Strangers offers a unique opportunity for reflection on one's life journey and personal experiences. It also affords a fresh perspective on how readers interact with others. The following discussion questions may be used privately to help journal the thoughts readers may have brewing during or after reading the book, and to provide insight into personal feelings the stories generate. Designed for book groups, study groups, and private journaling, the questions open the door for true discussion about matters regarding the power of story, spirituality, and how we may improve the world through more meaningful communication.

You can book River Jordan to visit with your book club through Skype, iChat, FaceTime, or by telephone. Contact her via e-mail at river@riverjordan.us. Please put "Book Club Visit" in the subject line.

DISCUSSION QUESTIONS

1. After reading *Praying for Strangers*, what did you feel impacted you the most and was your personal "take away" from the book? Has it affected the way you view or interact with people on a daily basis?

2. We often read books that seem to preach or that teach us ways we should think about our faith and about one another. How has *Praying for Strangers* helped you examine the lens with which you view yourself or the world? In what ways has it adjusted how you see those around you?

3. If you were to embark on this type of journey of the human experience, what do you think it would be like in real life? What are your concerns about what that might entail? What are your "wishful thoughts" of what that picture would look like?

4. Many people feel their faith is a private issue. Others are more comfortable with sharing thoughts regarding their faith in different ways. How do you feel about discussing your faith or the fact that anything faith-related is simply not a part of your life?

5. Although a very ancient word, one with powerful and universal meaning, the word *prayer* itself has become politically and emotionally charged—sometimes even divisive. How do you personally feel about the word *prayer*? What images or memories does it evoke for you? Has reading the book given you a different experience with the word? If so, how?

6. *Praying for Strangers* includes true-life incidents and people, and occurrences when River Jordan encountered people in her daily life. What stories did you connect with the most? Why?

7. Strangers in the book are simply people we don't know or haven't met—yet. How do strangers play a role in your everyday life? Do you have a story in which a stranger has come to your aid without your asking? Or a story of a time when you were able to help a stranger in a spur-of-the-moment happenstance? Did the experience empower your life?

8. Today's world and our real-life existence include many ways for us to connect with people through the Internet and social media. Do you feel these "advances" have helped or hindered our relating to one another on a human level? Why do you feel the way you do? Can you share examples?

9. We often wish to make the world a better place and to have some impact in our lifetime so that we may leave the world better off for our having been here. Do you believe this one tiny thing, praying for a stranger in your path, even if it's only a silent prayer, could make a difference?

10. Many readers relate that reading *Praying for Strangers* has greatly affected their daily communication with others. How has your

history of communication with the people around you been affected by reading the book? Are you more patient? More tolerant? Quicker to pay a compliment or offer assistance?

11. In reading *Praying for Strangers*, what has surprised you most in the story? What was the portion that you feel you would most like to relate to a friend? What would you tell your friend?

12. One of the continuing threads throughout the book is that a different person stood out every day as someone special to remember in a prayer. Those people came from all walks of life, all political parties, zip codes, faiths, and ethnic backgrounds. If you adopted this resolution for a day, would your choice of stranger be influenced by any preconceived notions? If so, why? If not, why?

13. If you have actually been inspired to start praying for strangers, what has been your experience thus far? How has it affected you? How do you think it has affected those you've encountered? Do you believe you'll continue this adventure of the human spirit?

14. If you had one blind, wild, wide-sweeping wish for the world today, what would it be? Why? What do you think it would take for that vision to come to fruition?

NOTES

NOTES

NOTES